Beyond Borders

Portraits of American Women from around the World

Dear Nigel
Thank you for your stories.
My Kunst

Photographs by My-Linh Kunst
Essays by Charlotte Fox Zabusky

Impressum

Biographies ©2008 by Charlotte Fox Zabusky
Essay ©2008 by Rosalind Williams
Photographs ©2008 by My-Linh Kunst

The book may not be reproduced in whole or in part in any form or by any means, electronic or mechanical, including photocopying, recording, or by any information storage and retrieval system now known or hereafter invented, without written permission from My-Linh Kunst.

Book design by René Winkler graphic design, www.dawinki.de

Exhibition curated by Rosalind Williams

My-Linh Kunst's photograph by Christoph Taterka

Printed in Germany by
Offsetdruckteam GmbH
Wegnitzer Strasse 1
58454 Witten
This book may be ordered on
www.AmericansBeyondBorders.com
or by emailing to My-Linh Kunst at
mylinh@kunst-photography.com

To my husband Matthias and my sons Manuel and Marlow

with my deepest love and gratitude. Without your support, patience and understanding, I could not have realized this dream.

To my mother

*with my admiration for your courage, strength and agility.
Like many of the women in this book, you became more of yourself
when you entered unfamiliar territory.*

Foreword

FAWCO is proud to be associated with this exceptional book "Beyond Borders: Portraits of American Women from around the World". As an international network of independent women's organizations with American and international memberships, FAWCO is no stranger to women who "make a difference" in a myriad of ways while living thousands of miles away from home.

Most members of FAWCO clubs are people who have moved abroad, and in establishing lives in their adopted countries, have used their time, energy and talents to enrich their families, communities, and therefore themselves. We feel privileged that 30 of our members are highlighted in "Beyond Borders".

This book is a tribute to the adaptability, inventiveness, and perseverance of these American women, who along with millions of other women just like them, believed they could "make a difference" in the world……..and did. Congratulations!

This book should serve as an inspiration to anyone moving abroad and to young people being educated overseas. Most importantly, this book shows the impact that individual people, each with their own unique ideas, can have in the world. Hopefully the stories in this book will inspire you to use your innate talents and ideas to fulfill your dreams, no matter where you live. Go for it!

Celeste Brown
FAWCO President
2007-2009

Introduction

My-Linh Kunst

Beyond Borders contains a collection of portraits and stories about cultural identity, about being an American woman in a world that has lost its belief in the good will of the United States, about the power to go beyond borders and make things happen, and about the necessary sacrifices and well-deserved triumphs along the way.

It's also a story of my personal development as a photographer. I'm a Vietnamese-born American. I'm married to a European and I've been living as an expatriot for more than half of my life. Whenever I land in a new town, my first port of call is always the American women's clubs. I find the instant camaraderie comforting as I navigate my way through unfamiliar places. For my first book, it seems fitting to profile the group that I've come to know so well—American women living abroad.

Very little is understood about this group of pioneers. Many of us follow our husbands to coveted overseas posts, or we fall in love with someone from a different country and find ourselves abroad. Some of us once had high-powered careers in the USA, but now we struggle to utter a simple sentence at the local grocery store. We reinvent ourselves and start new careers, because to practice our previous professions seems impossible due to language barriers, laws or cultural differences. We give birth in hospitals where the medical staff speaks little English, we dread the times when our bilingual children request help with their homework. Our ears perk up when we hear English spoken in the street, and we are drawn to other Americans who remind us of the place we still call home. We cope, we survive, we flourish. Some of us even manage to make a difference in our new communities.

Beyond Borders came together very quickly. Within a year, the project went from its initial conception to a published book and touring exhibit. I suggested the book idea at the FAWCO (Federation of American Women's Clubs Overseas) annual conference in March 2007. Charlotte Fox Zabusky, a published writer and FAWCO member, was introduced to me and agreed to be part of the project. All the stars became aligned when I met Rosalind Williams, a 26-year-veteran curator of photography. With her enthusiasm and encouragement, the project turned into a reality.

The following month, my request for nominations went out to the 15,000 members of FAWCO. By July, thirty women had been invited to be in the book. They come from twenty cities in fifteen countries around five areas of the world. The next four months were a blur of air travels and photo shoots. I traveled a few days every week, causing my husband to develop a new respect for single parenting as he steadfastly took care of our two young children. During that time, I suspect he went beyond a few borders himself.

I spent one day photographing and interviewing each woman. Each of these days was memorable in its own way. We normally composed a lifestyle portrait in her environment (home, local park, office, etc.) and a studio shot in front of a backdrop, where the women were encouraged to show their personalities through gestures or props. We talked, we laughed ... a lot; a few times, we cried. Except for Jean Darling, who, I felt, was completely in her element in front of the lens, most of the ladies were a bit self-conscious at the start. But as the day progressed and we got to know each other better, I could feel my subjects becoming more relaxed. As Phyllis Michaux said at the end our session, "I'm going to give you a smile now, and that's a big compliment to you." She crossed her arms and smiled big. I snapped the shot and that was the one selected as her portrait.

After the photos were done, we would sit down for a cup of tea and the women would tell me their stories. With some, we started with their life abroad; with others, it made sense to focus on the reasons they were nominated for the book; with a few, we would meander through their whole life. Having been part of the selection committee, I had preconceptions about each person, but these proved to be almost always not quite correct. There were elements of surprise in each of their stories. Sometimes, I was surprised by the impact of their feats, and how they surpassed my expectations. Other times, I was struck by the multi-faceted lives of many of the women – they were nominated for one reason, but turned out to be accomplished in so many other areas. And in some cases, I was surprised by their inspirations, or their insecurities. But what was consistent throughout the stories was that these women all have amazing conviction, resilience and agility. They have the conviction of their goals, the agility to know how to get there, and the resilience to push on in the face of challenges.

With many of the women, I got to know their families and to see my subjects through their eyes. I went to Wisconsin to photograph Krissy Capriles during her visit home. Her Dad chauffered me around and served as my lighting assistant; her beautiful 12-year-old daughter gave me a private performance of a touching, original song. But it was meeting her son Shane, a good-looking young man – whose autism had changed Krissy's life and enabled her to achieve all that she has for autism in Curacao – that left the deepest impression on me. Even though Krissy, a professional singer, knew how to work with the camera, I decided to use the shot of her and Shane. It's obvious that being a mother is the most important role she plays.

I journeyed to Casablanca to photograph Donna Sebti and Stella Politis Fizazi, two best friends who have been living in Casablanca for over 40 years, both humanitarians, who have positively touched the

lives of many in their local communities. Donna and Stella generously shared as many aspects of their lives as possible. I was delighted to have a typical Moroccan family couscous lunch with Donna and her husband, their four children with spouses, and their nine grandchildren. Stella took me to her Greek Orthodox church to hear her sing. I visited the 80-bed rehabilitation center that Donna helped create and the very British Churchill Club where Stella is the first American president. These are just examples of what amazing lives these women are living.

I have fond memories of visiting Jayne Cabanyes at her second home in Segovia, where a Roman aqueduct lands in her backyard. The house, with its peeling paint and crumbling foundation, needs major restoration, but it felt so warm, so full of distant voices and faces from the past. At one point, I thought I could hear the walls whispering their stories. We spent a beautiful day there. When I left, I felt as if my camera had captured a piece of history.

I photographed five women in Paris. My long weekend there during the biggest transit strike in the city has to top the travel hardship list; waiting hours for taxis that never came, then fighting millions of people in the Metro with my bulky equipment in tow. But the bruised shins and frazzled nerves were worth it once I got to spend time with Kim Powell, whose powerful features gave me my cover image. Phyllis Michaux read my palm, Kathleen de Carbuccia impressed me with her intelligence, Lucy Laederich astounded me with her passion, and Judith Barret touched my heart with her gentleness.

I remember my day with Shirley Kearney in Basel, Switzerland, strolling through the city and being shown its hidden treasures. I recall my dinner with Sara von Moos' family and how her two children entertained us with their stories. I am still laughing about my own hilarious private performance of "A Broad Abroad" by Gaby Ford, in the cosy hall where her theater group performs. I remember my midnight massage with Yuzana Khin after our long day's work in Bangkok. I reflect on my first visit to Helsinki, meeting the gentle Pearl Lonnsfors and helping her to be comfortable being photographed without her wig. I cherish the day I spent with the elegant Marjorie Gunthardt and her husband Hans. After our day together, she thoughtfully continues to send her words of support and encouragement to me by postcards whenever I need them most.

I remember my day with Robin Meloy Goldsby at a castle in Germany, where the world seemed to be spinning around us. Because we live in the same town – Cologne – I scheduled Robin to be my last shoot as a kind of celebration. But after three months of traveling and lugging my equipment onto planes, trains, and automobiles, my back gave out. Rescheduling was not

possible, so the night before the shoot I took a muscle relaxer, crawled into bed, and hoped for the best. Wide awake at three a.m., covered in sweat, nauseated and dizzy, I realized I had also contracted a stomach flu. But somehow, I got through the shoot. As long as I was looking through my camera lens, everything was fine. The second I stopped, the nausea and dizzyness came back. Now you know why Robin's portrait is a bit slanted.

I spearheaded Beyond Borders because I believe that the stories of these thirty inspiring women deserve to be told; they are a small sample of stories from women like them — American women living abroad and making a difference in the world around them. Because of my background, I am a person who travels beyond borders. I understand, respect, and admire what that means. I've chosen to focus my work on the people I know best — people who live beyond borders of nationalism, racism, age-ism and sexism, people who are capable of crossing over, contributing, absorbing, and learning from other cultures.

Each Beyond Borders woman showed me her strength, her courage, and her very American positive and can-do spirit. As a mother, wife, photographer, and citizen of this big, challenging world of ours, I know there will be many other borders to cross in my life. I will carry the images of these women with me for inspiration.

Essay

Standing Tall: We're All in This Together.

The seed for this project was planted during an international women's conference in Lyon, France, in 2007. When the workshop speaker touched on the topic of book publishing, My-Linh Kunst – the photographer – and I, seated close to each other, whispered, "Let's talk during the break!" Each of us knew of the other's profession – she, a photographer and I, a curator of photography exhibitions.

Those words were the first steps of an ambitious project – a published book and a travelling photo exhibition. As a photographer, My-Linh had long harbored the idea of publishing a book of photographs about women. The idea of a touring exhibition would only enhance her concept. I was thrilled to be onboard to help her bring it to fruition.

Before returning to our respective hometowns – Cologne, Germany and Madrid, Spain – we brainstormed and produced – in embryonic form – what would become *Beyond Borders: Portraits of American Women from Around the World*, the photographic book and accompanying exhibition.

At the outset of our endeavor, we asked ourselves some critical questions: Why? What? Who?

Tackling the why, as an American women living abroad, I have always believed in famed Swedish sociologist Gunnar Myrdal's phrase, "American Creed" – an expression of the conscious awareness that the United States is the 'home of democracy, liberty and opportunity.' Nearly 250 years after the Declaration of Independence was adopted by Congress, I considered it an integral part of our undertaking that we provide evidence of that American Creed in the day-to-day lives of women and the international cultures on which they have an impact.

Then came the what. What subject matter would we select for our show, for the publication? To find her portrait subjects, My-Linh secured the collaboration of the organization that had brought us together, the Federation of American Women's Clubs Overseas (FAWCO).

With 78 clubs in 38 countries and a network of 15,000 members worldwide, FAWCO proved to be a rich source for subjects to photograph for the book and exhibit. Ms. Kunst then established the criteria for selecting the portrait nominees: American women who were members of FAWCO, are living abroad, and have applied their considerable skills in their professional and/or social lives to "make a difference" through one or many activities performed in their adopted countries.

In the meantime, American writer Charlotte Fox Zabusky was invited to join the team as the biographer of each woman to be featured in the book. With the core creative and project management team was in place, nominations began streaming in.

After an overwhelming selection process and much deliberation we agreed on thirty subjects. We found our unique women in twenty cities and fifteen countries from five areas of the world – Europe, the Americas, Africa, Asia and the Caribbean.

Over a period of several months, photographer Kunst traveled the world to portray and interview each of the subjects. The results are powerful. With exquisite skill she presents a variety of photographs, with each woman basking in her own unique surroundings: a cramped apartment, a spacious home or castle, a public space, a garden, a park, a beach, a river bank, to mention only a few of the sites of the numerous photo shoots.

Ms. Kunst has produced work that holds true to the demanding criteria expressed by the great American portrait photographer, Richard Avedon:

One glance at these photographs reveals how Ms. Kunst very astutely conveys the essence of what each subject chose to communicate about herself.

Beyond Borders: Portraits of American Women from around the World, is a visual essay intended to represent the many American women who have, for one reason or another, left the United States for a residence overseas. These women have remained faithful to their American culture while embracing and skillfully navigating the cultures of their adopted nations. In these heady days of bi- and multi-culturalism, the women portrayed in Beyond Borders represent ordinary people who have accomplished the extraordinary, by adapting and contributing to their new communities.

Like many other American women living abroad, the Beyond Borders women have chosen to leave behind fulfilling lives and often lucrative careers. They've accepted the challenges of living and working in a foreign land, and, at the same time, have allowed their individual talents to shine.

Wading through layers of multiple cultures in today's shrinking world these women chose to stick it out. They serve as examples for present and future generations of women of all nationalities in similar situations. Through their courage, will and strength of mind they stand tall to make a difference. Why? Because we're all in this together!

Rosalind Williams
Independent curator specializing in photography
Madrid, Spain

"A photographic portrait is a picture of someone who knows he's being photographed, and what he does with this knowledge is as much of the photograph as what he's wearing or how he looks. He's implicated in what's happening, and he has a certain real power over the result."

Evidence 1944-1994 Richard Avedon

Acknowledgments

Acknowledgments

My heartfelt thanks go to Rosalind Williams for her belief in this project from the very beginning and her encouragement to pusue it; to Charlotte Fox Zabusky for her personal investment, dedication and volunteerism to complete the essays; I know there were times when we wanted to call it quits, but thank you for sticking with me.

Also my thanks to René Winkler for his beautiful book design, Pamela Gerla for supporting René, Silke Schäpers for volunteering to print manage, Lisa Schulz for donating her considerable talent and time to the website, the FAWCO Excecutive Board 2007-2009 for enabling me to tell the stories of these FAWCO ladies, Nancy Thornley for her help in the selection process, Robin Goldsby for her encouraging edits, Paula Daeppen and Joann Connel for their hospitality, Marjorie Gunthardt for her words of encouragement which always seemed to arrive just when I needed them the most, and last but not least, to all the ladies featured in this book for their inspiring accomplishments and to their family members who fed me, drove me, and assisted me during my short visit.

> *"Resolve to perform what you ought.
> Perform without fail what you resolve."*
>
> Benjamin Franklin

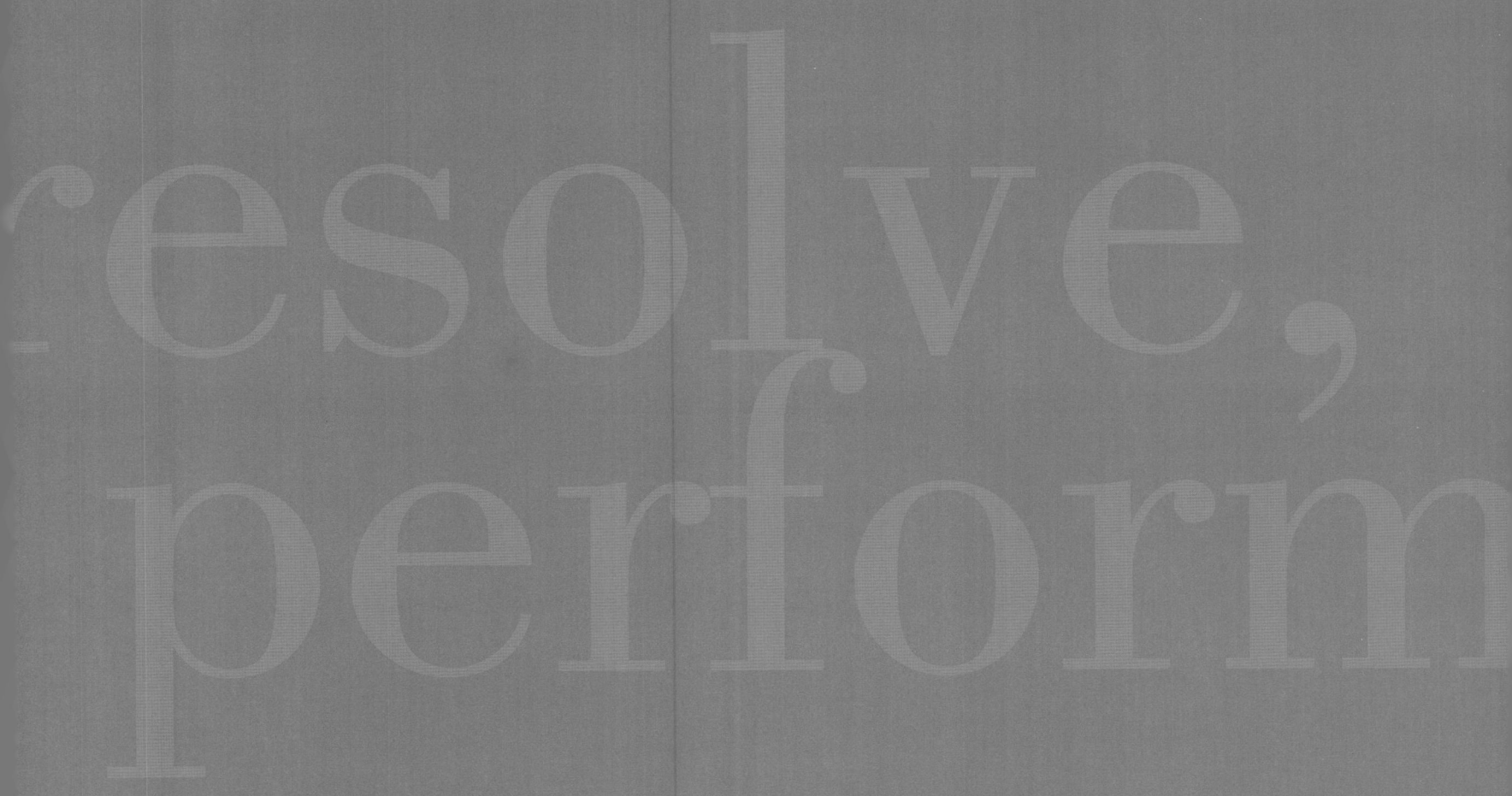

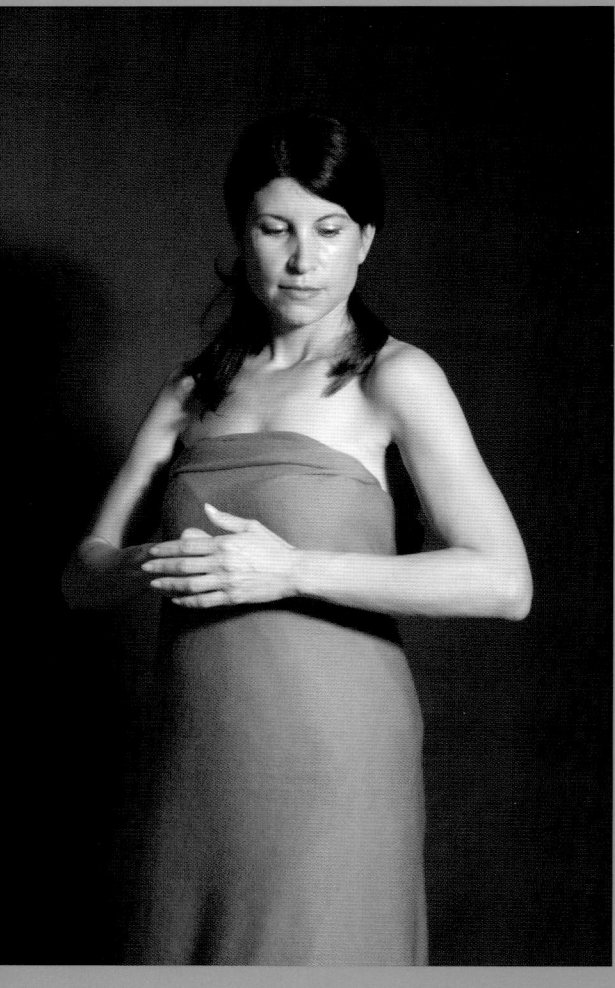

Márcia Balisciano

Business and Arts Executive,
Founding Director of Benjamin Franklin House
London, England

MÁRCIA BALISCIANO lives in London, where she is a business and arts executive and founding director of Benjamin Franklin House. She holds a PhD from the London School of Economics and began her career in London 12 years ago. She is a consummate businesswoman and is engaging, bright, confident, and reserved. By her own admission, Márcia is an alpha personality type, always "striving to achieve goals. I have but one life and I want to do something good with it."

Her idol is Benjamin Franklin because "he reinvented himself, didn't let obstacles stand in his way, and made lasting contributions." She is also inspired by "women leaders who achieve big things by doing what they love," citing Madonna and Madeleine Albright as examples.

She is most proud of her family and opening Benjamin Franklin House in London, an important transatlantic heritage site, to the public. Creating a landmark and thriving museum out of a forgotten house that Benjamin Franklin lived in for nearly 16 years on the eve of the American Revolution, brought her back to her American roots, and for this Márcia is grateful. It opened in January 2006, Franklin's 300th birthday, and, as Director, she is working to ensure the long-term future of the House and its educational aims.

For recreation and fun, Márcia has run marathons, completing seven in seven cities for seven causes. This successful businesswoman first moved abroad for educational and professional reasons, but is now likely to have a more permanent expatriate life with her French husband. She hopes to make further contributions over time — no doubt with her dedication and drive, she will.

Accept reality as it is and not as you wish it would be.

Helen Bannigan

Business Executive, Mother
Rome, Italy

HELEN BANNIGAN considers herself a "work in progress." She finds balancing work as a business executive and family a constant challenge – she works as Chief Operating Officer of a public relations firm while being a loving and supporting mother to two small children. Helen says that meditation helps. It is meditation that defines her approach to life, and it is meditation that first "opened her eyes to the value of life."

Helen craves to make a difference in the world, in business, in her community, and in human interaction. She has been doing just that ever since she first decided to backpack around Europe soon after graduating from college with a degree in Political Science and never came back. She studied in Paris, earned a Masters in French Foreign Policy and Diplomacy at the Sorbonne, moved to Lisbon to work for the American Embassy, and then, with a friend, started a telecom business there. Also in Lisbon she was one of the founding members of Grace, a non-profit organization dedication to raising awareness of socially responsible business practices.

Eager for more adventure, Helen moved to Spain, met her future partner, and her life once again veered in another direction. With the love of her life at her side, she moved to Italy, and they have been living in Rome for the past seven years, acquiring two children along the way. There she founded the Rome chapter of EuroCircle, a network of European and international professionals.

Helen speaks several languages, has lived in several countries, and "in her spare time" does free-lance work in cross-cultural training for international business executives transferred abroad. After close to two decades of experience in international public relations and European telecommunications, she is now Chief Operating Officer of a technology-specialized public relations firm. Always, Helen's business motto has been: Only progress that is ethical is genuine.

In spite of this fulfilling and successful background and current work in business, Helen considers her most important job to be raising her children to lead "full, joyful lives of intent and integrity." She brings them weekly to a shelter for victims of human trafficking where they play with the children of the women housed there, to show them both how fortunate they are, and that they are just the same as kids living in different circumstances all around the world. Her guiding principal has always been to "live life with intent, not by default," and she hopes to inspire her children and those around her by living by those principals every day.

*Whatever you do,
try to do it to the best
of your ability.
It is the only way
to achieve quality
and satisfaction.*

Judith Barret

Teacher, Founder, French International School in Hong Kong
Paris, France

JUDITH BARRET, a Californian with undergraduate and graduate degrees in Hispanic American Studies and Education from Stanford University, received the Palmes Academique, the highest award in French education, and is listed in the French Who's Who. With a French husband and three children (one born in Algeria, one in San Francisco, one in Madrid) they set out to work in the world. Originally, Judy had wanted to go into the diplomatic service, but married to a French graduate student that was not possible at the time. Flexible and adaptable, she created a new future for herself, learning French and earning a teaching degree. During several international moves because of her husband's career in banking, she worked as a teacher; she taught Spanish, French, history, English and special education. While living in Spain she was involved in the creation of the first International Women's Convention and represented the US. The development of the FAWCO "Peace Through Knowledge" program there became a theme in her life and work as she co-founded a Spanish educational center for children with special needs and worked on the embassy's Spanish-American Cultural Board.

In Hong Kong she established, with some other parents, the French International School there in 1982. Finally, back in France, she continued to teach English, history and special education in schools with international sections both public and private, and especially enjoyed serving as a mentor for students in the Model United Nations program in Paris, Bath and at the Hague until she retired to spend her time caring for her husband who had become disabled. Judith then became an administrator of SPRINT, Sharing Professional Resources, Ideas and New Techniques, a non-profit professional organization for children with special needs, founded in 1986 by a group of English speaking and bilingual professionals who work with children of all ages who have special needs. Her commitment to excellence in education, her positive and can-do approach to life, her enthusiastic and enterprising work on behalf of others have had an impact on her family (each have entered international fields and have furthered international comprehension and cooperation) and on the many children whose lives were enriched by her efforts on their behalf.

Have fun, be happy and make others happy.

Marcia Brittain

Advocate for Breast Cancer Early Detection
Montevideo, Uruguay

MARCIA BRITTAIN says "Do your monthly check, and get your annual mammogram." She expects that her friends in Montevideo will remember her as the one who was always saying, "Think of me when you get squeezed." Marcia's humble and quiet air belies the dynamo she is when it comes to accomplishing great things - for example, her groundbreaking work for improving breast cancer awareness in Uruguay.

Marcia gave up her job as airline costumer service agent to follow her husband on their first expat tour – Montevideo for three years. They are the parents of three young children, and her life in Montevideo centered around the children's activities and her own connections with the American Women's Club. In conversation with a local doctor, she was shocked to learn that breast cancer is the second cause of death among Uruguayan women due to lack of early detection and follow up, along with proximity to public facilities providing cancer care. Marcia wanted to do something where she felt it could really make an impact regarding awareness and treatment toward this deadly disease.

A simple fundraiser idea gained momentum and support from the American Women's Club and the diplomatic circle, raising in its second year $12,000 for the cause. This type of fundraising event, begun by an American expat's commitment, was a first for Uruguay and has now become an annual event to raise money toward Breast Cancer treatment.

"This all ties back to my mother." Marcia's mother died in 1990, from breast cancer, because Marcia believes, she was afraid of the pain and mutilation of the surgeries and treatment. Sure that many other women had the same kinds of fears, Marcia's focus in Uruguay was on raising awareness for early detection and treatment.

Her efforts have resulted in the donation of a portable sonogram machine to help surgeons simultaneously view and remove the disease. The American Women's Club's purchase and donation of a new Johnson & Johnson hand-held Mammotome Breast Biopsy System, a first of its kind in Uruguay, has been provided for by the public health care system of Uruguay.

Soon it will be possible for a mobile unit to travel to the interior of Uruguay to provide mammogram services, and if needed, diagnostics and surgery in a matter of days rather than weeks or months.

Back in the U.S., Marcia's next stop will be to further educate women about the present non-invasive breast cancer surgery techniques with an emphasis on early detection. Her goal is to remove the fear women have of the treatment. This expat has made a solid contribution to her temporary country and an important difference to hundreds of its women.

¡Que me quitan lo bailado!
(They can't take that away from me!)

Jane Cabanyes

Cross Cultural Activist
Madrid, Spain

Widowed some thirty years ago, JANE CABANYES is 92 and chose her husband's family home in Segovia as the site of her interview. With its 15th century walled courtyard and garden in which the last arch of a 2,000 year old Roman aqueduct is embedded, it offers a respite from Castile's relentless summer heat. The house, however, represents only one aspect of Jane's life in Spain.

Jane grew up on the North Shore of Chicago, her father was an engineer, her mother a college professor of Latin and biology. After graduating from Mount Holyoke, she was sent to the US Embassy in Madrid while working in New York during World War II. Few women started their professional life working for the OSS, which became the CIA. It was so secret that after their 1947 wedding, she never even told her architect husband, Cayetano Cabanyes, about her life in espionage.

Although never quite achieving a complete osmosis into the lifestyle of a typical señora madrileña, she gracefully navigated a balancing act adapting to the role of a traditional wife in Spain with her work as a picture researcher stringer for American Heritage and Horizon.

Jane also devoted her time to volunteer work, the hands-on American style of volunteerism. For twenty years she actively served on the Board of Madrid's Anglo-American Hospital and periodically on that of the Instituto Internacional (International Institute) a privately funded organization, dedicated to providing women, access to formal education, contrary to Spain's then-existing custom, and to foster cultural exchange between Spain and the US.

During the politically sensitive 1950's era in Spain, Jane used using her low-key, diplomatic style to help the director of the Instituto Internacional resist pressure from its US-based Board, composed mostly of intellectuals from Spain exiled in New York, which was insisting on the Institute's administration issuing an anti-Franco statement. Given that a government ordered police raid of the premises had already taken place, such a communiqué might have undoubtedly resulted in the closing of the Institute. In those pre-Internet days, at Jane's skilled insistence, eloquent letters flowed between Madrid and New York and eventually the Board's request was dissapated.

Those who know Jane consider her to be active, peaceful, cultured, persistent but patient, and above all, resilient. Of herself, she says she used to be feisty and daring. She still enjoys life and loves to travel, in particular to the Middle East and Morocco. An avid gardener in her beloved Segovia, a voracious reader and enthusiastic bridge player, a music lover from opera to jazz, and with her fluent Spanish she keeps a foot in both worlds, that of her native country and that of her adopted country.

Disability is just another word
  for different abilities.

Krissy Capriles

Singer, Autism Advocate/Fundraiser
Co-founder of Autism Association of Curacao (AAC)
Curacao, Netherlands Antilles

KRISSY CAPRILES is enthusiastic, energetic, and eager to talk about her passion- autism awareness, and support for children with autism and their families. A lively, young woman who began singing professionally at the age of 15, she first went to Curacao as a singer/dancer with a New York Revue, met her Antillean husband two weeks later, and they've been inseparable and living in Curacao ever since. She continued singing professionally, during which time, she and her husband established a production company to bring international performing acts and events to Curacao. When her first child, Shane, was diagnosed with autism at the age of three, Krissy's life changed dramatically and she shifted into high gear to learn and do all she could about autism, which became her focus in life. Today, she is proud to be the "poster girl" for autism. She first educated herself, then went looking for other parents who were facing the same fears and challenges, and soon thereafter, helped establish a support group for families with children on the autism spectrum. Prior to that time, the disorder was barely even heard of on the island of Curacao, and there was little help, or support at all for the families. Krissy gave them hope. Her message was: "No matter what, we won't lose hope." Whenever she visited her family in the U.S., she took advantage of the time there to meet with autism experts and to learn more. Then, in 1998, with "a handful of loving, caring parents," the Capriles founded the Autism Association of Curacao, (AAC) dedicated to raising awareness, giving information, enabling early detection, and supporting therapy, education, creating housing options, and integration for people living with autism. Largely through Krissy's activism, the AAC became a dynamic association that will be celebrating its 10th anniversary next year. Soon thereafter, Krissy's work began in earnest – contacting respected experts in the field from the U.S. and Europe and inviting them to come and lecture at workshops in Curacao, and Aruba, helping to organize an important and successful symposium, as well as initiating numerous major fundraisers in both Curacao and Aruba for the cause. From a parent's point of view, she has been asked to speak at an international autism conference, and has written well received articles. She is known to be always readily available to help desperate parents of autistic children find proper placement for their children's special education needs. She still looks back at herself in amazement, saying, in her exhuberant voice and with her characteristic smile, "Now, how did this little girl from Waukesha, Wisconsin ever have the guts to do something like that?" Asked to identify herself, Krissy says she's got a great sense of humor ("Humor carries you through in all situations") and she's "found meaningful purpose" in autism ("Music was my passion; autism is my mission"). Indeed. And so Krissy Capriles "a girl from Wisconsin," became a woman from Curacao, an expat who made a difference.

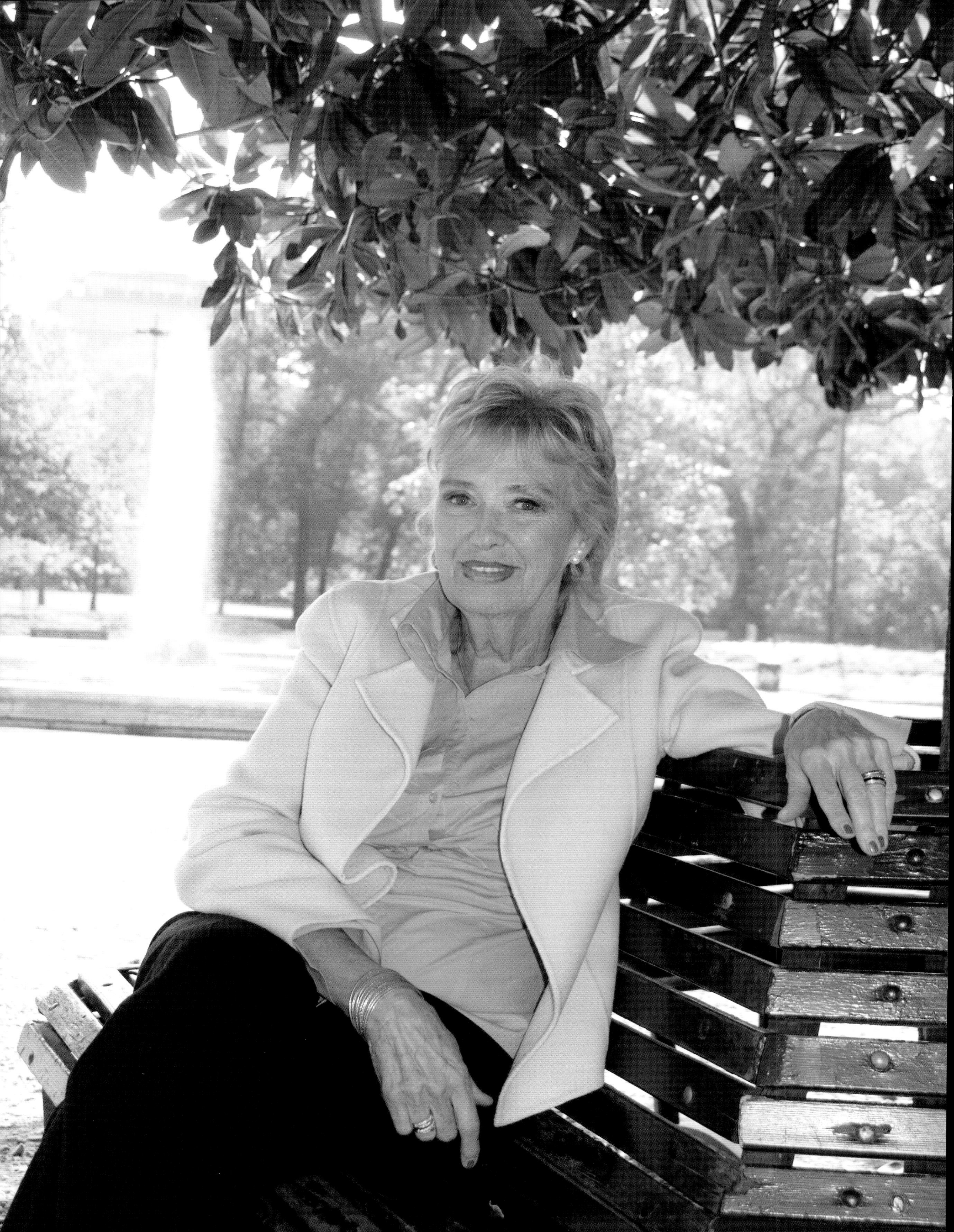

If at first you don't succeed, try, try, try again.

Barbara Cocchini

Entrepreneur
Milan, Italy

BARBARA COCCHINI is a role model for many professional women in Milan because she was one of the first expat women to successfully establish a company in this city, an unusual and innovative feat at the time in the 1970s. She founded the first expat relocation agency in Milan, is still active in it, although her son has recently taken over management of the company.

Barbara is a graduate of Middlebury College and has a Master's degree from Harvard University. Before coming to Italy 36 years ago, she was a successful career woman in the US, having been on the Harvard faculty of research, a consultant for New Jersey State Commission for the Blind; and, in New York, a Fulbright Analyst, Middle East Specialist and head of Overseas Programs Division of the Institute of International Education-administering Ford Foundation and Rockefeller grants.

She received the Lifetime Achievement Award from the expatriate community in Milan in recognition of the many groups of which she has been a founding member and officer: Americans in Milan, International Marriage Group, British American Nursery, Professional Women's Association, English speaking theatre group to name a few. She served on the International Advisory Board of WIN conference and the U.S. Consulate's Community Leader's Group. For her accomplishments in business in Italy, Barbara was elected to "International Who's Who of Professionals" in the year 2000 and has recently been inducted into the Rotary Club of Milan.

Still starting new professional projects at her age, she inspires hope in young professional women, who tend to reach out to her as a mentor. One young friend wrote "She is more than an inspiration, she is a pioneer of entrereneurship, a powerhouse of business not to mention a prodigy of a musician, who communicates not only through words, but through her amazing actions, proves that there are no limits to what one can do! She blesses the lives of many in endless ways and deserves to be recognized for her amazing contribution to Italians, Americans, and the International community."

Friends her own age consider her elegant, warm, creative and energetic, although she believes people see her also as bossy and possibly too self-assured. On reflection, she thinks they're probably all right. She would like people to see her vulnerability as well as her defenses, but realizes that it would depend mostly on their projections. She feels she is essentially a happy, optimistic person who likes to solve problems.

She now devotes most of her time to volunteer work, and to playing the piano. In fact, Barbara stresses that, more than role models, music is the true inspiration in her life. She is proudest of her therapeutic work with the blind and of her accomplishments in her careers and her company, her piano playing and in the fact that her son has told her he had the happiest childhood of anyone he knows.

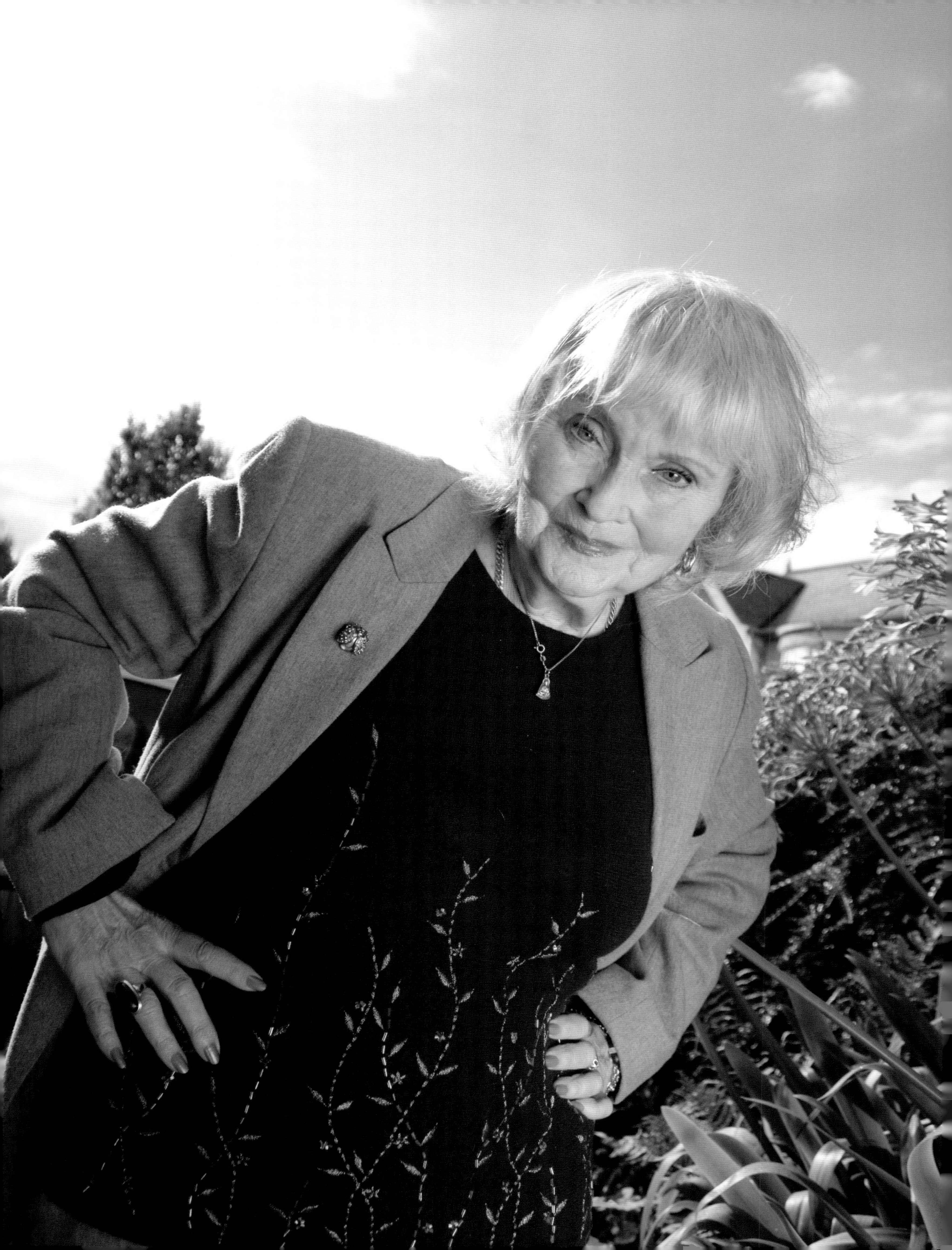

Not to mourn what is lost, but to enjoy and make the most of what I have left.

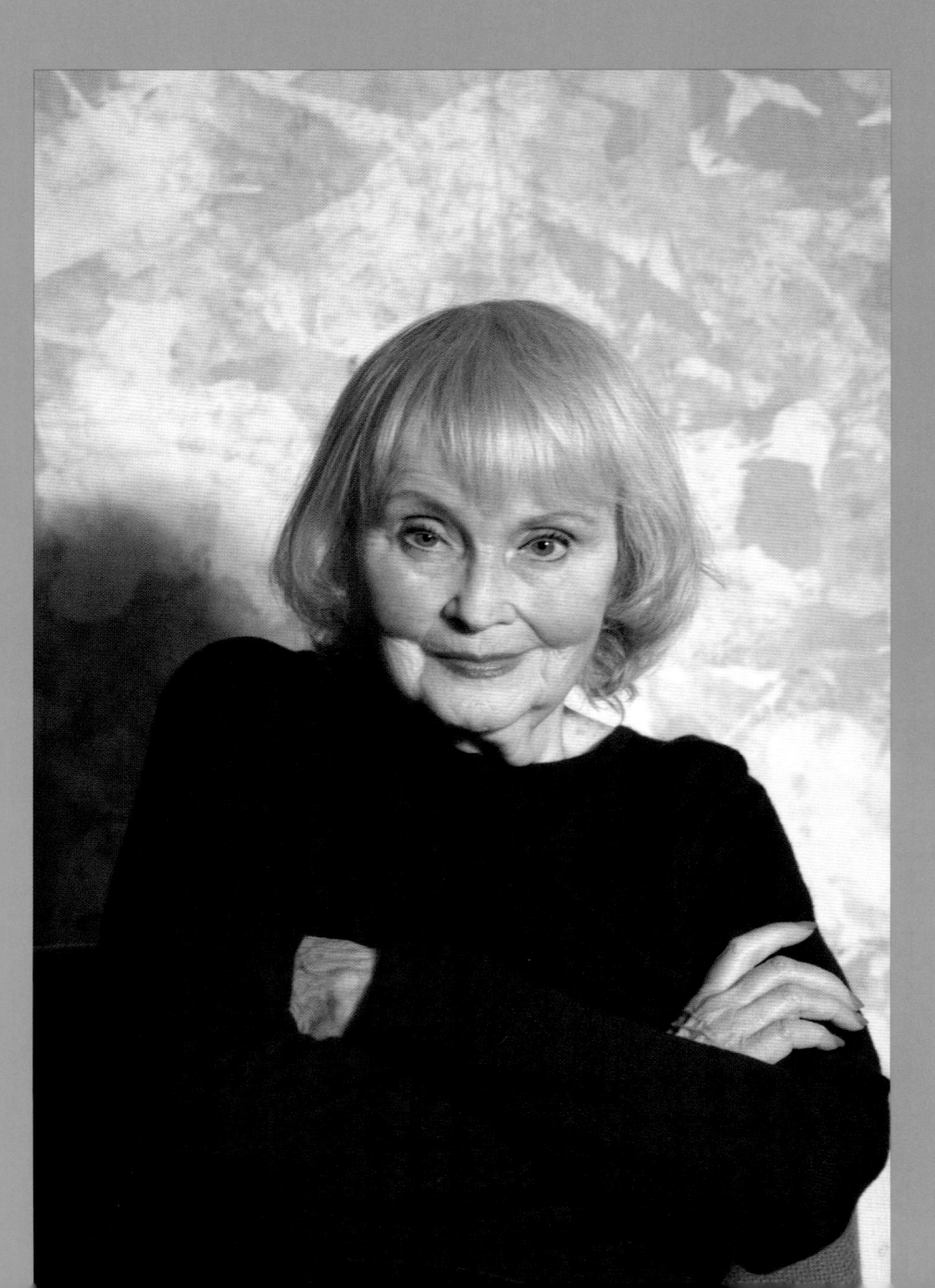

Jean Darling

Actress, Author
Dublin, Ireland

JEAN DARLING, 85 and living in Dublin, is a show business veteran and still acting, both on and off the stage. Although she'd been in movies since the age of six months, you may remember her as the only little girl in the Our Gang Comedy series in the 1920s and 30s. She has written a book about that time, "A Peek at the Past", published in 2003. After leaving Our Gang, she toured vaudeville in a single act until, in 1945, she played the part of Carrie Piperidge in the original Broadway production of Carousel, and, in fact, played 850 consecutive performances. Later, she traveled around the world in her magician husband's show, Magicadabra, as a singer. When he suddenly disappeared – he has subsequently died – they were performing in Ireland, and she decided to settle and raise her son there. She subsequently reinvented herself by writing short mysteries, for Ellery Queen, for Alfred Hitchcock, and for Mike Shane Mystery Magazine, as well as horror fantasy stories for Whispers Magazine. For eight years, she played Aunty Poppy in a very popular and long-running children's show on radio and television in Dublin, during which time she wrote 450 stories for the show. She is still recognized by children on the street, who run after her, shouting, "Auntie Poppy, Auntie Poppy." Always ready to reinvent herself as needed, when an accident blinded Jean for a couple of years, she gave singing lessons. In a serious accident 14 years ago, Jean's spine and leg were destroyed, and the doctors told her she'd never walk again. Never daunted, she took up yoga, practiced every day for two years, and began to walk again. Jean has never felt homesick and never felt lonely. She has a "travel" bear, which she takes with her wherever she goes, because "home is where the bear is." She loves the sea and loves to sail, and try as she might, she just can't stay angry. It's just her nature, she says. Jean calls herself a "ditzy dame" and says she's "very good in bad situations, very sensible." She's also funny and has a wicked sense of humor. Asked what inspires her, she replied, "Being alive - and I like it this way." Asked what defines her as a person, she replied, "Who knows?" Asked what she hopes her portrait would reveal about her, she replied, "What I look like." But she answered honestly the question about her proudest accomplishment: "Becoming a published author, something I wasn't taught to do." Cheerful, positive, optimistic, and forward looking, Jean summed up her life by saying she does not want to mourn what is lost but to enjoy and make the most of what is left.

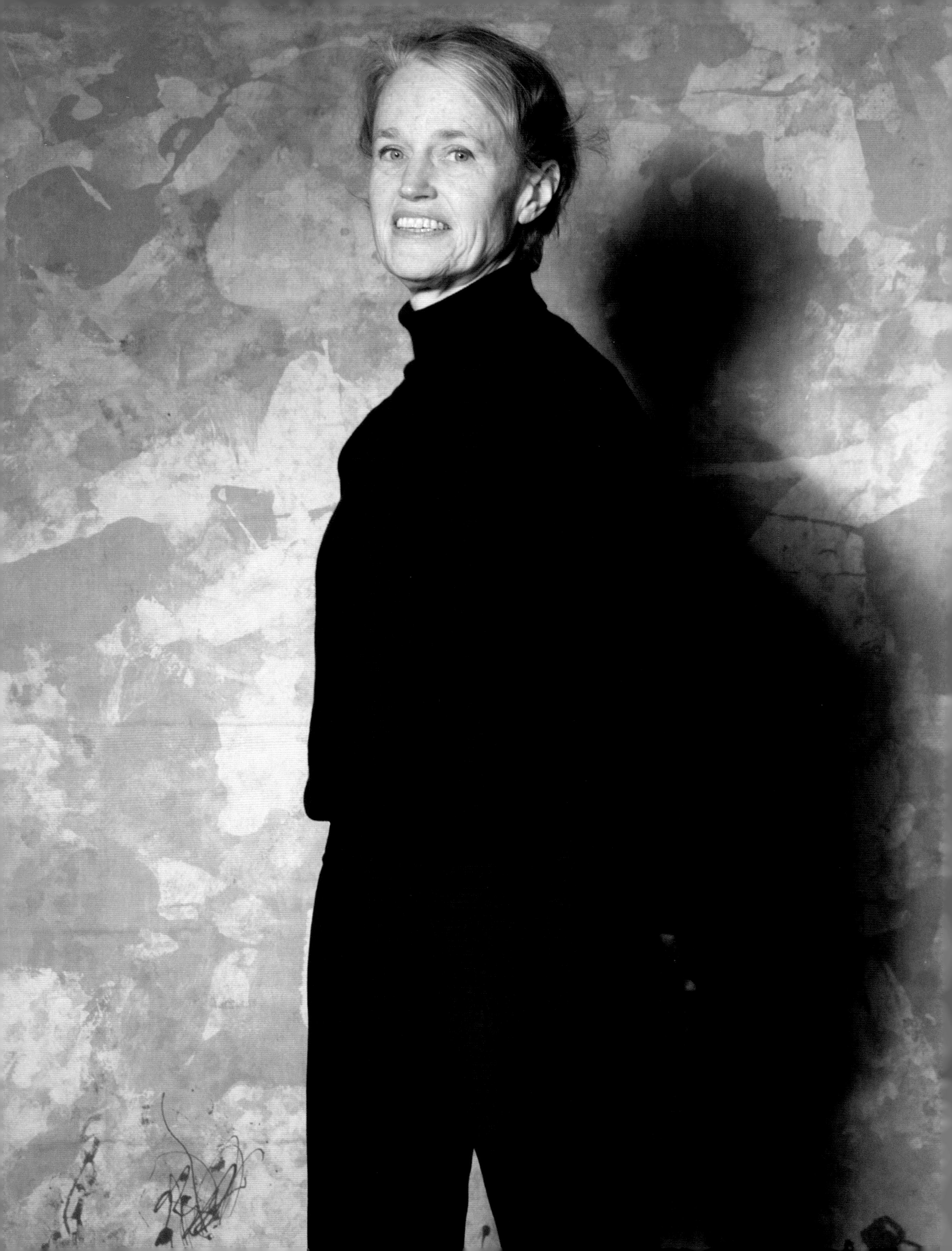

"Can hardly sit still when I think of the great work waiting to be done."

Susan B. Anthony at 80

Kathleen de Carbuccia

Diplomat, Lawyer, Advocate for Overseas Americans
Paris, France

KATHLEEN DE CARBUCCIA started her career as a diplomat, working in the US Embassy in Paris, until she met her favorite Frenchman and decided to give up her diplomacy career (a must if you work for the State Department) in favor of marriage, children, and a life in France.

She did all that, raised her children there, and then, at the age of 42, decided to reinvent herself once more,"...this time as a French and American lawyer". She went back to school, and passed the New York Bar the first time, while still living in Paris!

Kathleen is a great example of a bright, energetic, and competent American woman, able to make not only one but two new lives for herself in a foreign country. She is also active as President of the Association of American Residents Overseas (AARO), an organization that "gives a voice to Americans living abroad, whose role as "unofficial ambassadors" of their country is often overlooked. AARO actively educates Congress, the media and the public on such vital topics as taxation, absentee voting, citizenship, representation, Social Security and Medicare."

In her poised and elegant manner, Kathleen not only reaches an amazing level of personal achievements, but is also making a difference to all our lives abroad.

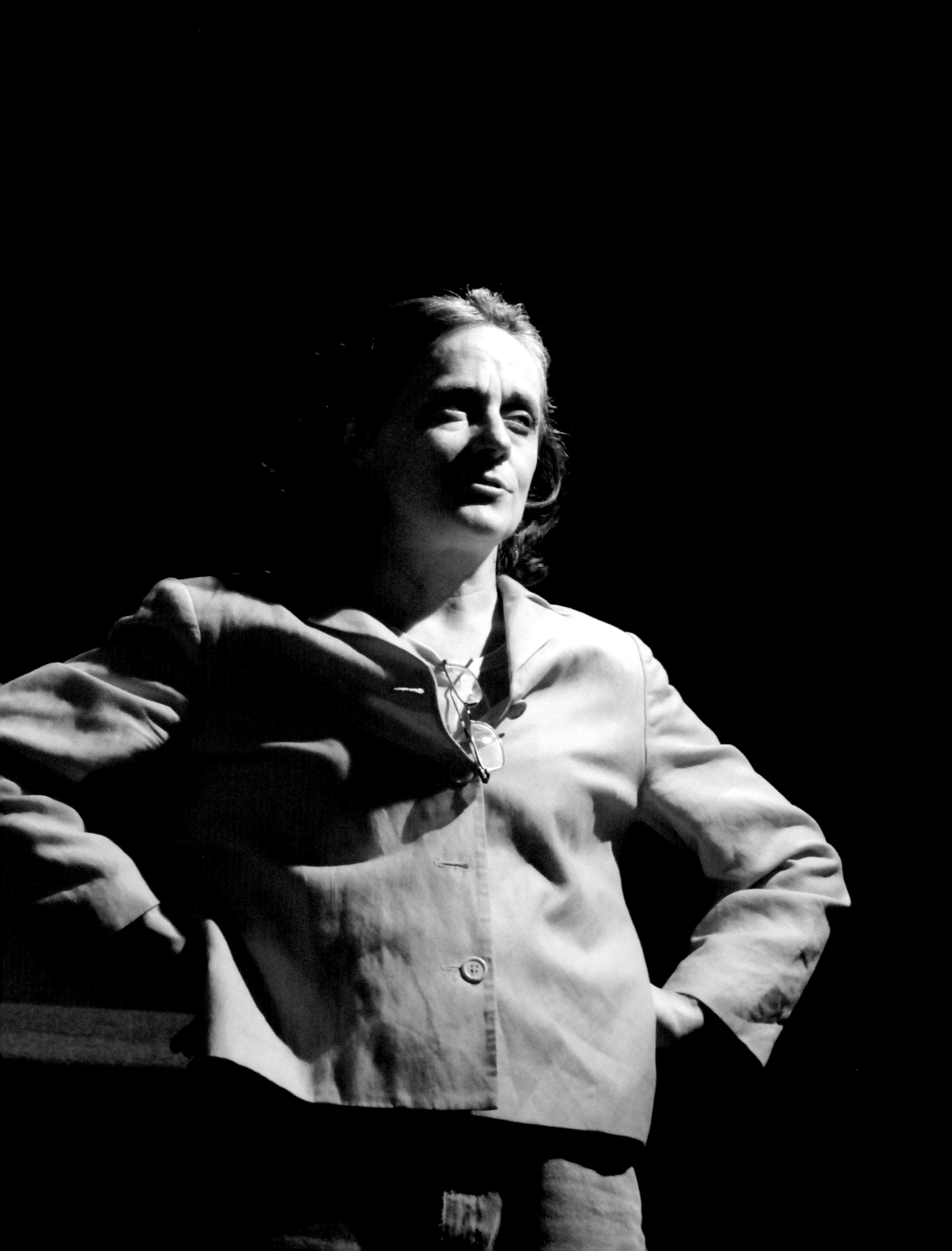

*Pursue your dream
and do as little damage
as possible.*

Gaby Ford

Actress, writer, director, producer, founder of The English Theater of Rome, GABY FORD is a down-to-earth, no-nonsense woman with a healthy lack of seriousness about herself and her work. Humor plays an important role in her approach to life. She calls herself "a rough, tough cream puff," and her own admitted goal in life is to do as little damage as possible. Originally a dancer, Gaby first came to Rome from New York, where she had been on a dance scholarship with the Alvin Ailey Dance Theatre, while teaching at a fitness club. Soon she found work as a character actress in film and television type cast as the foreign spinster. Since her first love was theater, however, in 1996 she opened her own English Language Theater, a repertory offering a wide range of plays from classic to contemporary, world premieres, and bilingual productions. In addition, directing and acting, she also took on the role of business manager, working through the Italian bureaucracy to keep her dream afloat. In the end, she was successful and is now a highly visible and well respected member of the arts community of Rome. She has forged connections with international schools, with numerous embassies, and with the United Nations, organizing theatrical programs at their request; she has provided free entertainment at the UN Women's Guild Camp for Handicapped Children, at Christmas parties for orphans; as well as raise funds for deaf children in Italy. The theatre has been instrumental in helping many actors and writers launch their careers; and highlights women's issues by showcasing women playwrights, directors, and film makers. Gaby herself writes mostly comedy and is, basically, a comedienne. She wrote and still performs a hilarious one-woman show, "A Broad Abroad." One of her hobbies is restoration and with the help of her father was able to obtain a country apartment in the magical 15th century town of Bomarzo and restore the walls, ceiling and beams by herself. This home has served as a "boot camp" for actors in rehearsal and offers a quiet space to playwrights. Within the first year two new plays have been composed there. She considers her most significant accomplishment to live simply and to have survived the creation of 64 productions through twelve seasons of The English Theater of Rome.

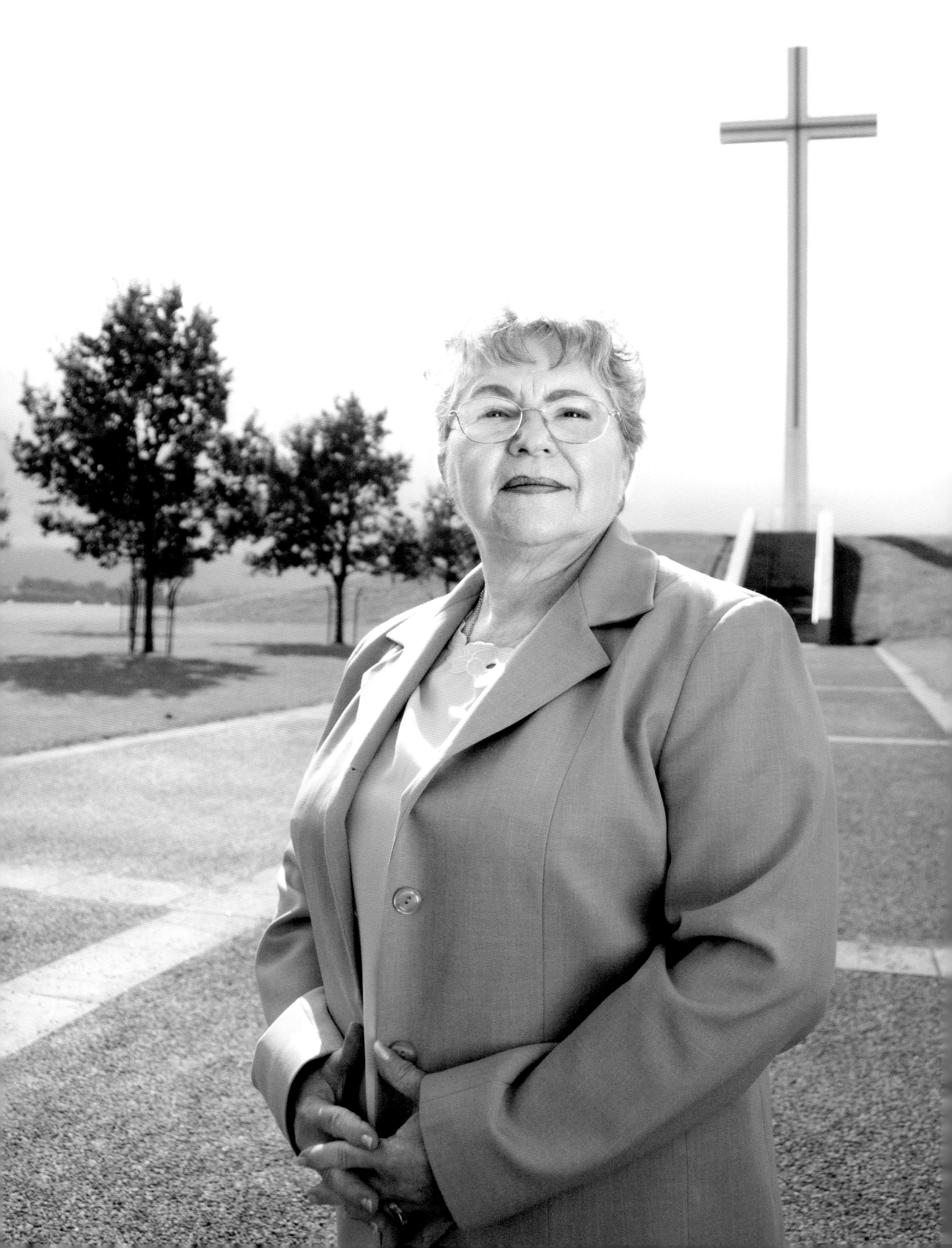

*Life is full of adventures and challenges.
Embrace it with all your heart.
Go forth bringing peace and love.*

embrace

Joanna Gallagher

Teacher, Ex-cloistered Nun
Dublin, Ireland

JOANNA GALLAGHER has written a long manuscript about her life as a cloistered nun, but she wants to edit it before sending it off to a publisher. Now that she's retired, this lively, 70-year-old expat in Dublin, who has enough personality for two, expects to have the time at last to do that. Joanna's history is unusual and interesting. She had been engaged as a very young girl but broke it off to join a convent in England, where she remained for 20 years. Always a rebel and a questioning person, after a while she began to question her role in the convent. She struggled with this question for a long time, praying that if God wished her to leave the convent He would have to open a way for her. When she received news that her father was terminally ill with cancer she asked for and was granted approval for a year's leave of absence. During that time she also traveled to several convents and researched their plans for renewal after Vatican II. She brought that information back with her when she returned to her convent in England. However her community was not able to survive and she decided she was not ready to die with them. Eventually, in her early 40's she married an Irish man who had been in the same religious Order and made a home with him in Ireland where they've lived now for over 30 years. Joanna and her husband had met when she visited Ireland on her return to England. Both had left their Religious communities independently when they met up again after her husband had returned from his work on the South African Mission. She is proud of her happy relationship with her Irish husband. Settled in Dublin, Joanna went to work in the prison system, as a teacher and as an organizer of educational programs and other projects to help juvenile offenders overcome their addictions and to use their skills for the benefit of society and themselves. She did this through facilitating "health awareness, good relationships, and the need to look at their own problems and find peace within themselves. She also used drama and music classes, such as basic guitar, script writing, performing. Joanna also believes in the power and strength of women, especially in their "fantastic" philanthropic projects all over the world. "Women are nurturers by nature," she says, "managers for their families. They are charismatic organizers because they have to be. And they have great compassion for the weak and the needy." She has been the Chairperson and National Coordinator for the Christian Feminist Movement, the Chairperson for Leaven, an organization for former priests and religious brothers and sisters and their partners, and especially involved in the National Council for the Status of Women in these past years as well as one of the early representatives for Fawco NGO committee to the United Nations in Geneva. Now Joanna is active in an Older Women's Network, dedicated to helping older women throughout Ireland and the EEU to become aware of their rights and entitlements and to live active and happy lives. She has always been interested in advancing women's issues, whether it be in society, in the Church, through neighborhood groups, or through international organizations. And always, she remains a person of strong faith.

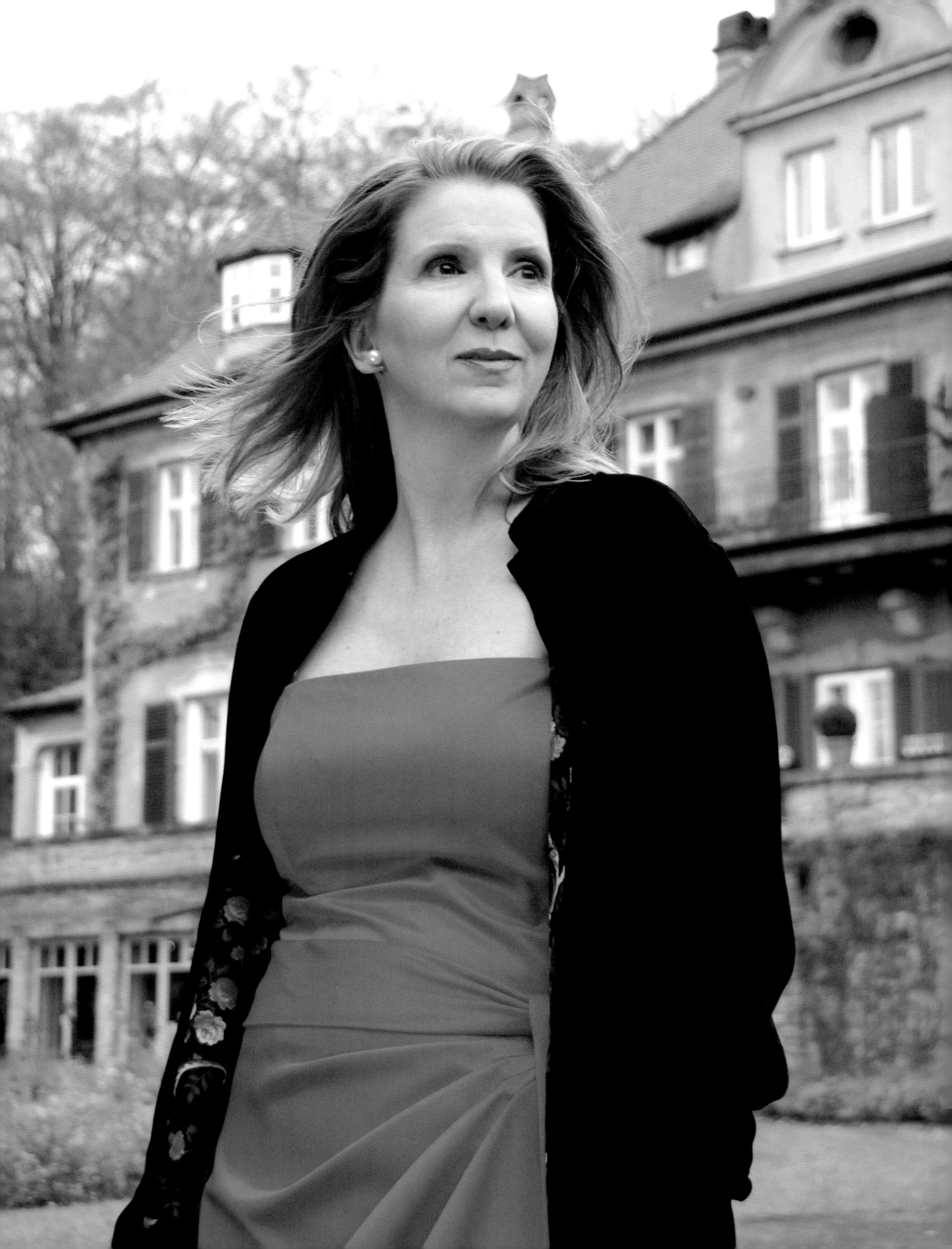

fragile

Life is fragile, people are strong.

strong

Robin Meloy Goldsby

Musician, Author,
Cologne, Germany

Pianist ROBIN MELOY GOLDSBY writes books, song lyrics, and music that sparkle with her enthusiasm for life's strange twists and turns. After working for more than a decade as a pianist in some of New York City's swankiest hotels, Robin followed her husband, world-class bassist John Goldsby, to Germany, where he accepted a position with the Grammy Award-winning WDR Big Band.

In the first years following her move to Lohmar-Wahlscheid, a sleepy village in the hills outside of Cologne, Robin negotiated the emotional obstacle course encountered by many of the women included in Beyond Borders. In Robin's acclaimed book "Piano Girl: A Memoir," she recounts, with a keen eye for the absurd, the everyday scuffles of trying to learn a new language and culture.

To take the edge off of her loneliness, Robin sat at her grand piano and began composing songs about her move to Europe and the friends she had left behind. This sensitive and inspirational work is included on Twilight, a solo piano CD popular on both sides of the Atlantic. Robin's latest recording, Songs from the Castle, mingles her graceful melodies with the poetic arrangements that have become her trademark. In addition to concerts and readings all over the world, Robin performs regularly at Schloss Lerbach, a castle located in Bergisch Gladbach, Germany, close to the home she shares with her husband and two children.

When Goldsby set out on her musical voyage of self-discovery she didn't know that her very American style of piano music would be one day be embraced by so many Europeans. "I've never set out to change the lives of the people who listen to my music. I'm just trying to play what I feel, one note at a time. A beautiful melody speaks a language that transcends our cultural similarities and differences. I've performed in concert halls, smoke-filled bars, third-world countries, and some of the world's most luxurious hotels. I've yet to find a place that couldn't benefit, in some small way, from honest music."

Robin's gentle determination to express herself through song invites her international audiences to tap into a different sort of American artistry - a reflective and radiant feminine spirit that represents American women with dignity, humor, and grace.

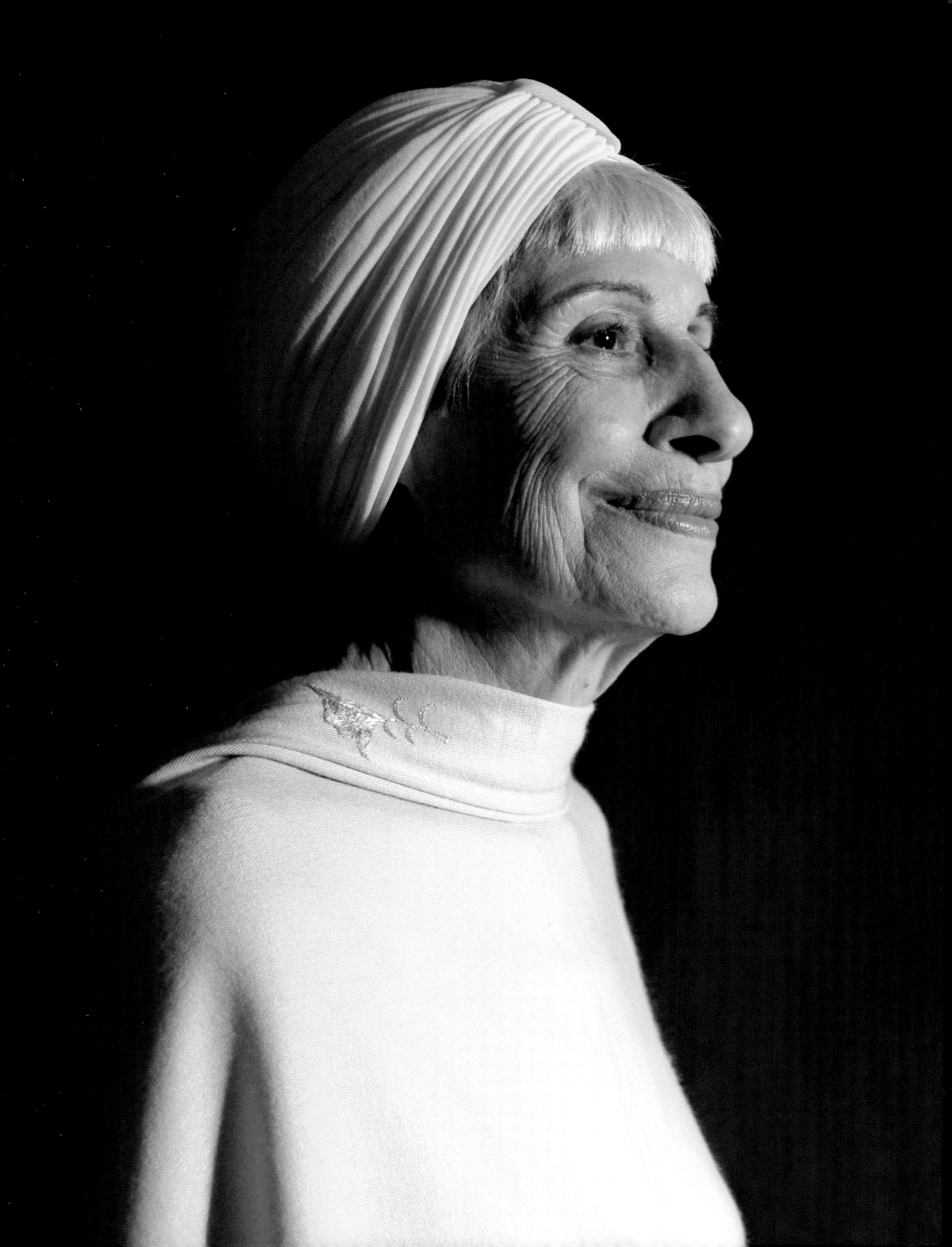

*Time is so precious,
we are only given
one minute at a time.*

one

A real, honest-to-goodness poet – that's what best describes MARJORIE GUNTHARDT, who began writing poetry when she was seven years old, in Arlington, Massachusetts, and is still writing poetry at the age of 85 in Zurich, Switzerland, where she has lived for 35 years, with her Swiss-American husband Hans.

Marjorie has a long and varied history in the arts: she wrote not only poems but also songs for solo voice, both the words and the music, and she won several first prizes for these in the Scholastic National Music Awards. She performed one of them on radio in New York City and was interviewed on air by writer William Saroyan. While studying on a Drama Scholarship at Emerson College, Marjorie won an Atlantic essay award, and was listed in Who's Who Among Students in American Universities and Colleges. She was invited to join the Bread Loaf School in Vermont, where she met Robert Frost and Truman Capote, and then went to the University of Colorado School of Journalism.

After World War II, Marjorie traveled with international students, in a converted troop ship, to participate in the first School of European Studies in Zurich. Back in the US, Marjorie worked in Boston then Washington DC, writing book reviews and poetry, and being an editorial assistant. When her husband died suddenly, she moved to Greenwich Village from Washington and went to work at the New York University Press.

Her life changed dramatically when she met a Swiss-American who fell in love with and married her, and, in 1963, moved her and their three sons to Zurich, where they have been ever since, except for some years in Massachusetts and Paris. In Zurich she became active in the American Women's Club of Zurich, were she started a writer's group, gave poetry programs, and began her life-long hobby of bringing Americans and Swiss together. Marjorie has been teaching English at the Berlitz School for 30 years. She is the oldest teacher there, but she has "young ideas."

Marjorie's first book of poetry was published in Switzerland, and she has recently completed her second book of poetry. She and her husband treasure their 52 years together in a happy and successful inter-cultural marriage.

Marjorie Gunthardt

Poet, Teacher
Zurich, Switzerland

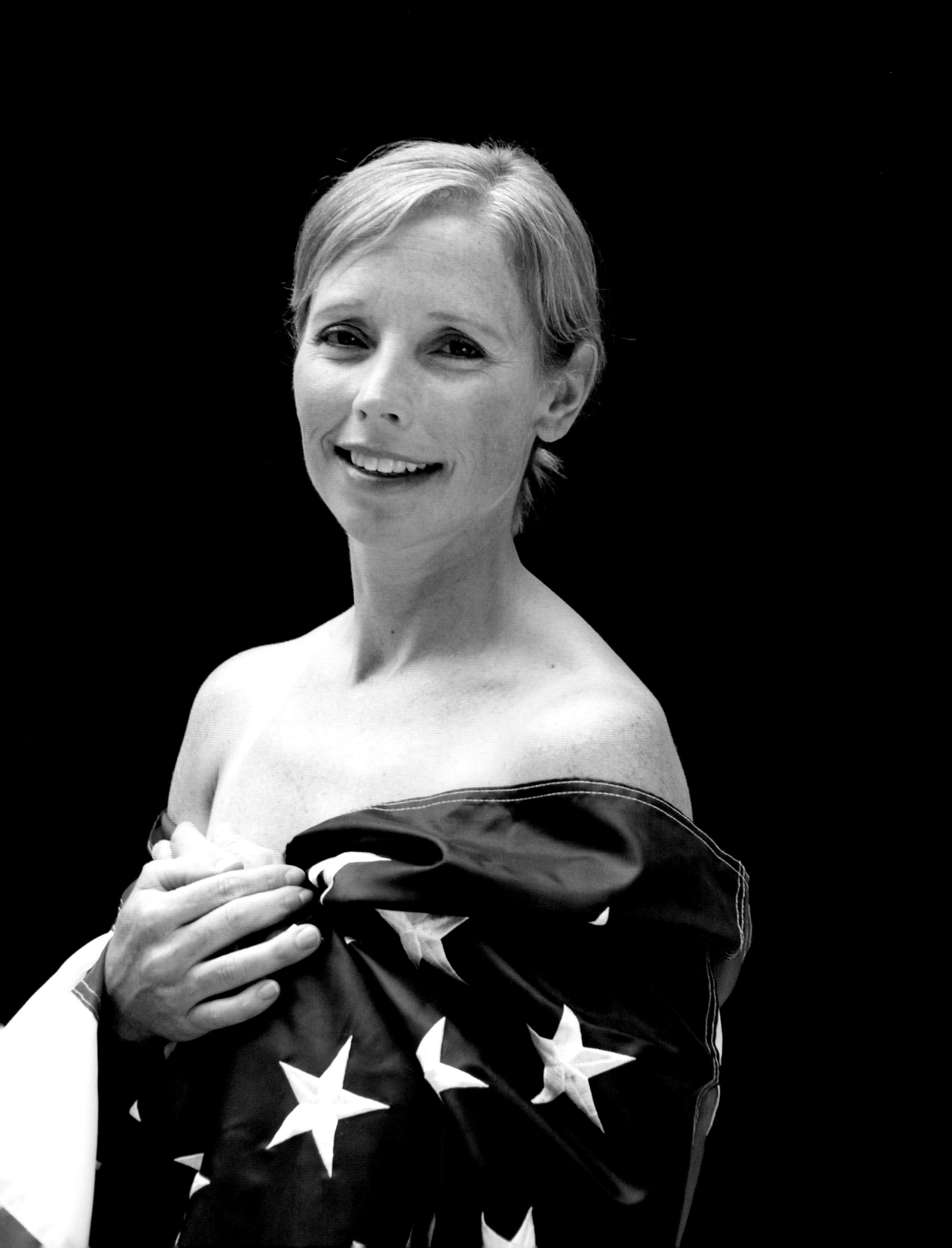

I am intention and want to do everything in life for God's intention.

Carol Hoag

Chemist, Expatriate Director for Love Without Boundaries
Shanghai, China

In January 2007, CAROL HOAG arrived in Shanghai on her first expat experience. The next month, she volunteered to become the Expat Director of Love Without Boundaries (LWB), a global organization providing surgeries to Chinese orphans, in order to give them better futures, to make them eligible for adoption, and in many cases to save their lives. A true baptism by fire – into the cultural life of an unfamiliar, and perhaps exotic, country and culture, and into the very satisfying life of an expat who makes a difference in a new place.

Quiet and reserved, gentle and genteel, Carol and her husband, the parents of two boys, had considered adopting a baby from China, but she became ill and they were unable to go through with this plan. Then, when her husband was offered an assignment in China by his company, the couple eagerly accepted the opportunity, and not only for professional reasons but also because they had both wanted desperately to do something else, something "beyond." Carol, a self-described deeply religious woman, says she "knew from inside" that there was a reason for her to be going, that there was something she was meant to do there.

That "something," presented itself almost immediately through a woman from her church, who took her to visit an orphanage and told her about Love Without Boundaries (LWB). The Shanghai chapter of LWB benefits from free surgeries performed by a generous local chinese GI and neurosurgeon, and some visiting American pediatric surgeons. Because about 30 babies come to Shanghai for surgeries during these weeks, help was necessary to organize and prepare for the doctors' visits. Volunteers were needed to pick up the children from the trains from all over China, and to visit the hospital several times a day to be sure there were enough diapers, snacks, clean laundry and love for each orphan and their accompanying "auntie". Carol was asked to become the Expat volunteers coordinator, she immediately took up the challenge to recruit and organize a group of expats. She continues today to coordinate the work of all the volunteers. Carol feels this work is "a calling," that it gives purpose to her life, that it has "become my job."

She is already afraid that it will be hard to go back home and leave the wonderful volunteers she's been working with – the doctors and the expats and the local Chinese citizens, people she might never have met had she not been willing to immediately plunge herself into the life of Shanghai. In fact, it is only the Shanghai Chapter whose volunteers provide this hands-on kind of volunteer work, and that is thanks to Carol Hoag, another example of an expat who made a significant contribution to her adopted country.

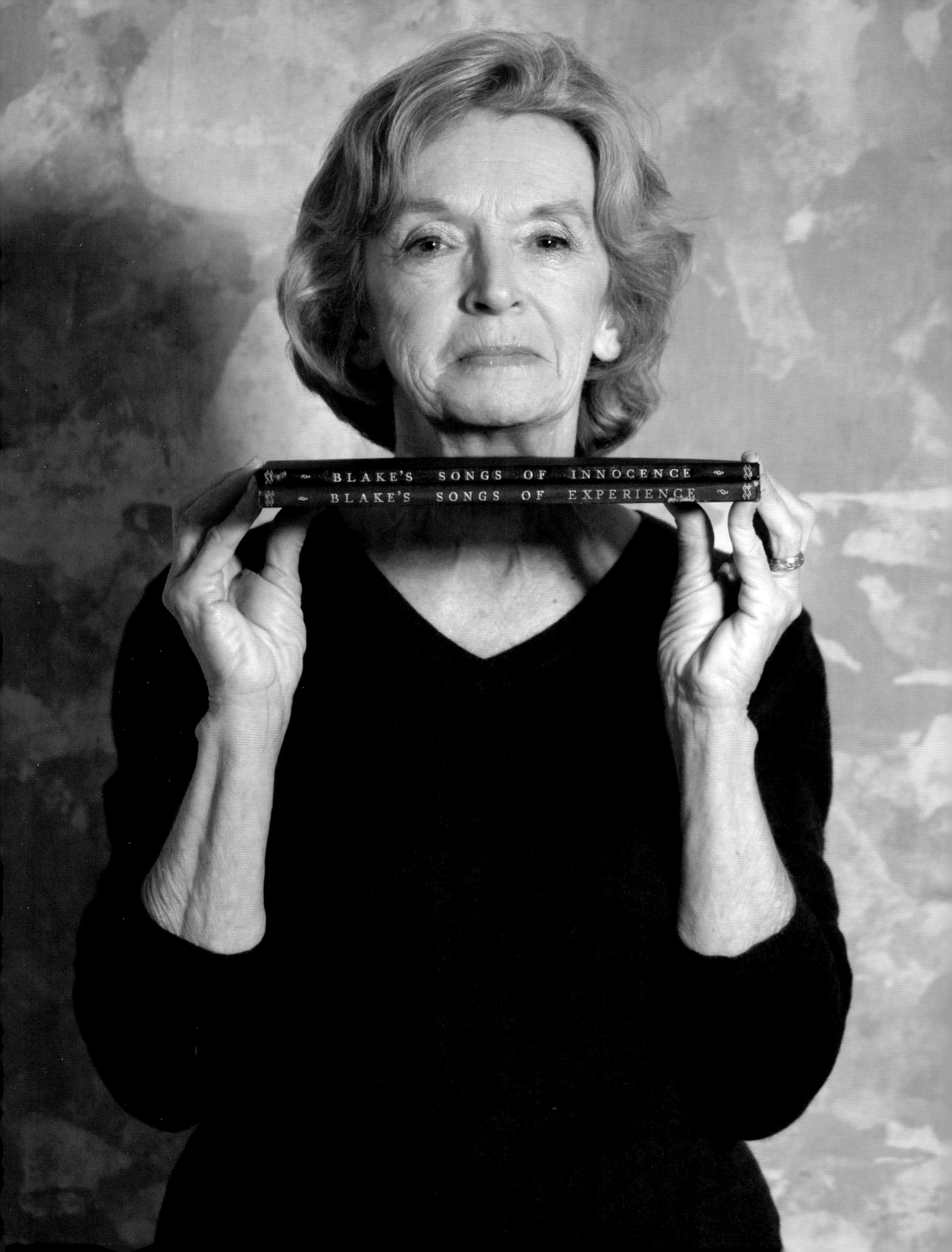
BLAKE'S SONGS OF INNOCENCE
BLAKE'S SONGS OF EXPERIENCE

You never know, until you ask or try.

Shirley Kearney

Author, Editor, Activist
Basel, Switzerland

"In 1970 we moved from the comforts of New Jersey suburban living to a sylvan fairytale setting in Lucens in the canton of Vaud, Switzerland, five years after the village celebrated its 1,000 anniversary." That's how SHIRLEY KEARNEY described her move to Europe. When their children were 8, 10 and 12 years of age,

Shirley and her husband decided they wanted to venture into a life outside the United States for a few years.

One child wanted to live in a castle, one near the mountains, and the other close to horses. During a business trip to Switzerland, her husband succeeded in filling all wishes: two floors of the caretaker's home at the Château de Lucens, perched on a hill overlooking the village, was to be their new home. At that time, the castle was owned by Sir Arthur Conan Doyle's son and was open to the public; part of it housed the Sherlock Holmes Museum.

Shirley and her family entered wholeheartedly into the daily life of a French-speaking Swiss village, though no one in the family spoke one word of French. The children went to the local school and Shirley earnestly began to learn French. It was to be an adventure, one that at times was disconcerting and humbling.

After two years, a decision needed to be made: return to the United States or stay on in Switzerland; the children voted to remain. The family then moved to Basel, where they were confronted with German and the Basel dialect. With her children out of high school, Shirley, who thrives on challenge, went into high gear. First, she was the Swiss representative for Earthwatch and participated in archaeological digs in Israel and in Neuchâtel. In Basel she collected cost-of-living data for a consulting firm and organized one-day seminars addressing issues facing expatriates living in Basel.

In 1986, with the assistance of two women, Shirley wrote, compiled, edited, and published a 48-page booklet, which turned out to be the first edition of "Basel: A Cultural Experience." At this time she was English-language editor for a number of books on banking, while in her vacation village of Charmey, did translations for the Musée du pays et Val de Charmey and worked on the first English version of the town's website. Meanwhile, the booklet on Basel evolved into a 272-page book; the new version was published in 2005.

Shirley is happiest when exploring Basel, on foot or bicycle, constantly on the lookout for local cultural treasures, issues or personalities on which to report. A journalist by nature, she writes articles for regional publications. An expat by choice, Shirley has become a voice of her adopted city, describing it and some of its less well-known pleasures to anyone interested.

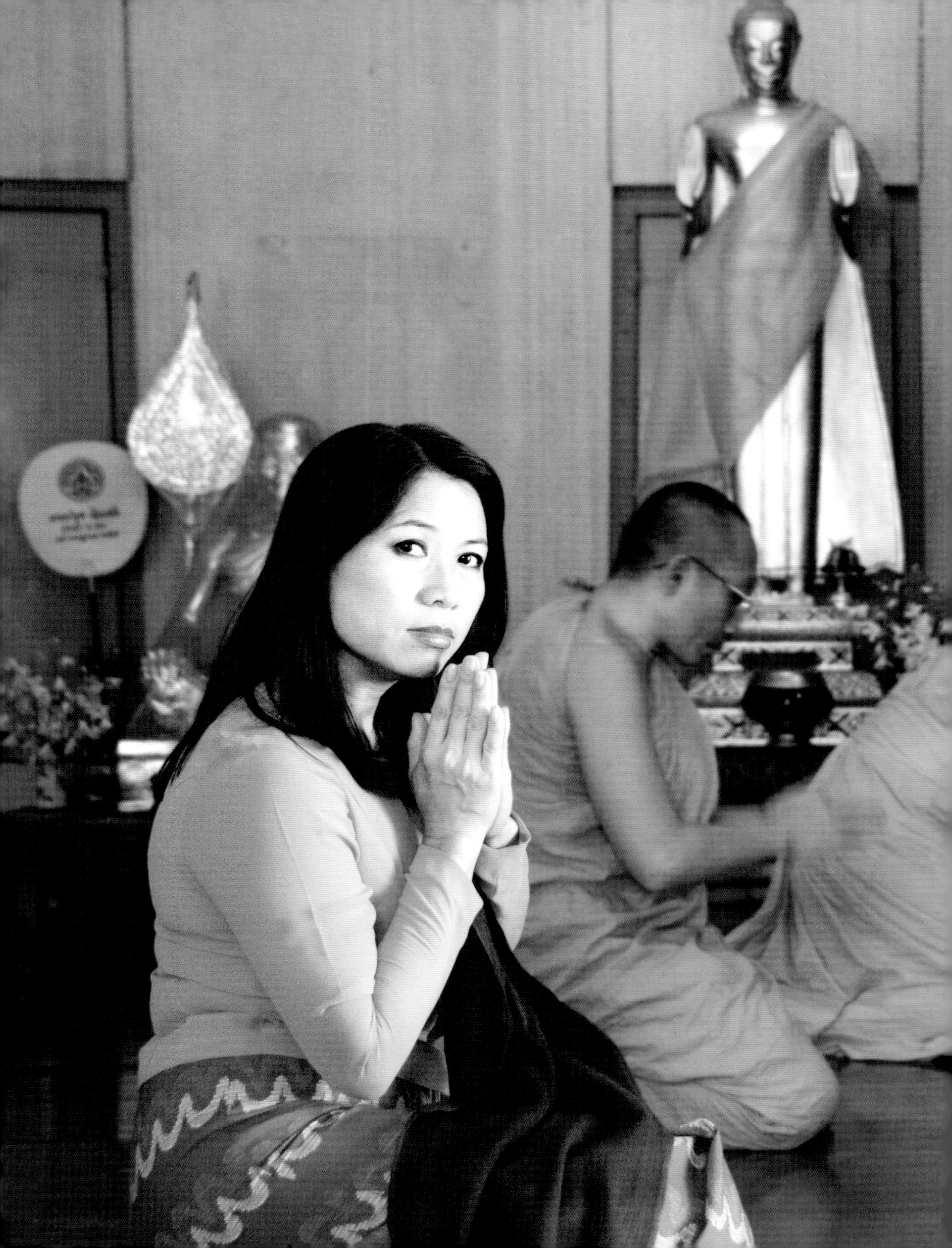

*"When I honor my father
I honor all those who stand for
Political integrity in Burma."*

Aung San Suu Kyi

YUZANA KHIN, a poster child for Amnesty International, has been a political activist since she was a student in Burma - studying psychology and already pursuing a career as a singer. She became involved in the pro-democracy movement of 1988, as a student leader she raised the consciousness of and offered support to those being oppressed by the government Junta throughout the country. After the government killed thousands of the unarmed student demonstrators and began searching for their leaders, Yuzana was among those escaping to Thailand to continue the movement on the international stage.

While the majority of students decided to take up arms against the government, she disagreed with their philosophy of meeting violence with violence. She strongly believed that what was needed was education and health, and thus, devoted herself to that goal, first assisting refugees fleeing from Burma by working with the Jesuit Refugee Service in Bangkok, and later, in the late 1980s, by taking on the roles of public speaker and performance artist in the U.S. to make Congress, the American people, human rights organizations, and the world aware of the crisis in Burma.

Yuzana completed her undergraduate degree in the U.S., toured with Amnesty International to raise the awareness of the plight of the people of Burma and then returned to Thailand, to work as Health Liaison Officer for the International Rescue Committee, serving the ethnic minorities from Burma in the refugee camps along the Burmese-Thai border.

She learned that she needed to know more about public health issues in order to help the women and children in the camps, and so she went back to the U.S. for a graduate degree in she also volunteered for NGOs and community-based organizations, assisting in the resettlement of the first Burmese refugees in Atlanta.

Now back in Thailand as an American citizen and wife of a diplomat, Yuzana spends most of her time caring for her young children and preparing to study for a doctorate investigating the issues faced by Burmese women workers trying to access health services in Thailand. Although her life has taken a 180 degree turn, the plight of her native countrymen and women remains central, and she continues to support the Burmese refugee and migrant communities in Thailand.

Yuzana Khin

Human Rights and Health Advocate
Bangkok, Thailand

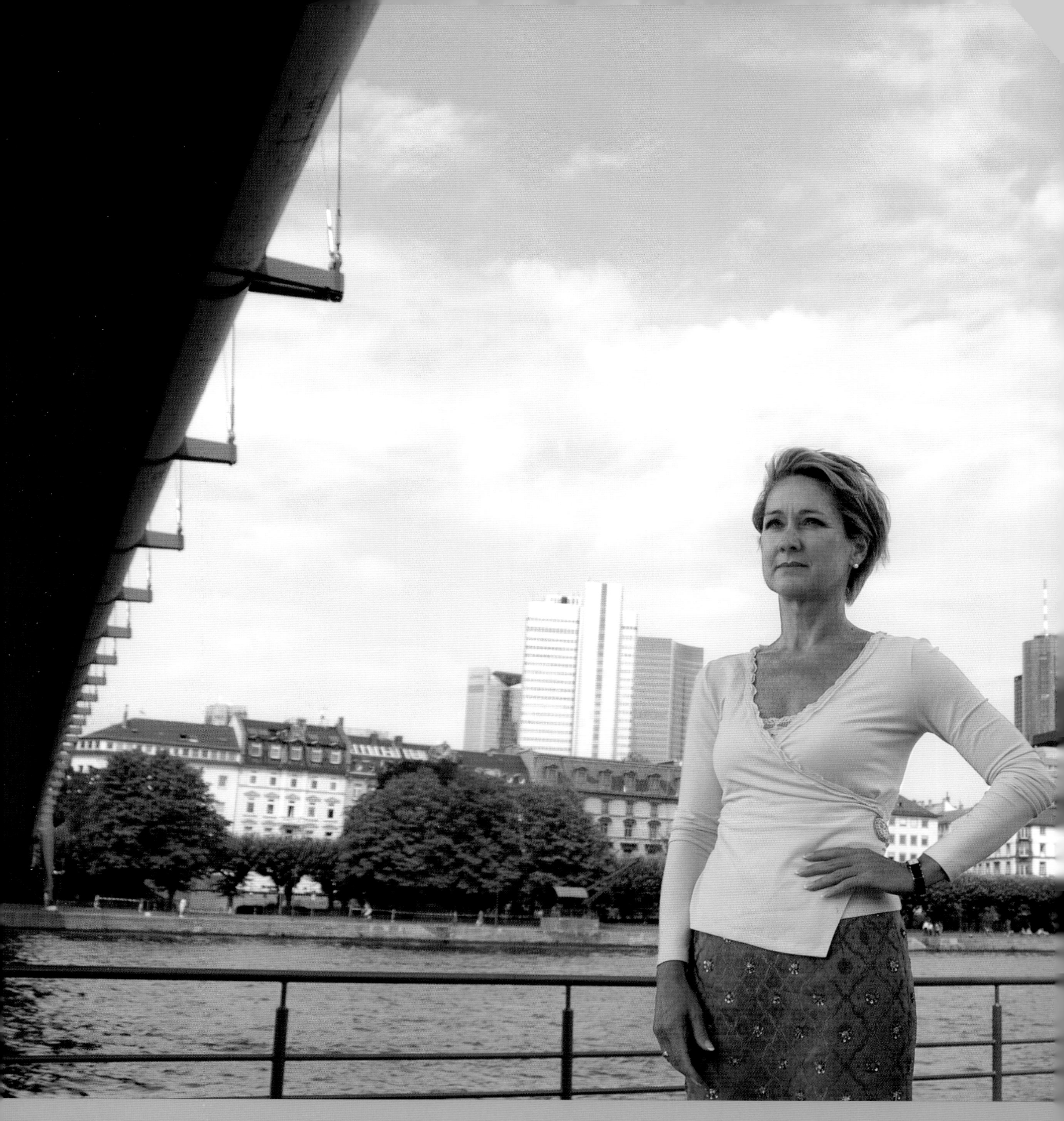

„Whatever you can do,
or dream you can do,
begin it.
Boldness has genius,
power and magic in it."

Goethe

Cheryl Koenig

Entrepreneur
Frankfurt, Germany

CHERYL KOENIG is a firecracker, to quote the photographer My-Linh Kunst, who took these fabulous pictures of her. She is full of personality, poised, and completely professional. Her motto is "Just do it," and do it she does and has: "[When I first came to Germany] my world as I knew it came crashing down. Because I couldn't speak a word of German, I became deaf and dumb overnight. I was a very self-confident, independent woman who had "made it" in New York City and London, and here I was in Frankfurt and couldn't even make a call to arrange for my own hair appointment! I had completely lost all self-confidence. I was afraid to drive anywhere for fear of getting lost, so I sat at home alone day after day, feeling completely cut off from the world." And that's when she came up with an idea that might have saved her that lost time. She founded a relocation company because she instinctively knew that there had to be a market for helping other "poor, helpless souls like myself."

She was right. That company grew to be such success that her German husband gave up his own work to run the business with her. Cheryl says people think she's tough, but she thinks that's because she will go through fire for both her clients and her team of loyal employees and consultants, always. We think she's an example of an astute American businesswoman who becomes a success in a foreign country because of her realization that, in her own words, "you are responsible for your own happiness," wherever you may be.

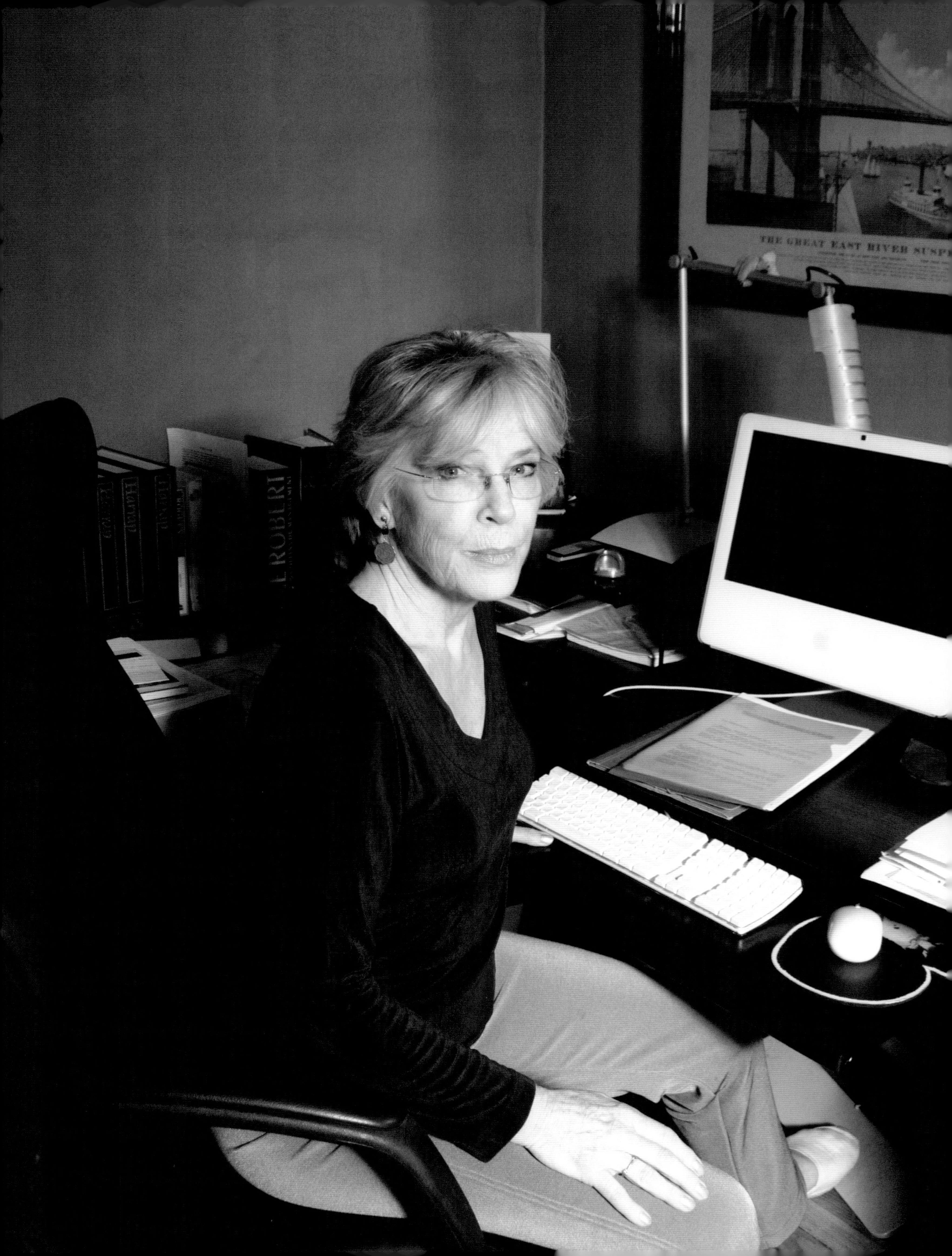
THE GREAT EAST RIVER SUSP

"*As life is action and passion,
it is required of a man that he share
in the passion and action of his time,
lest he be judged not to have lived.*"

Oliver Wendell Holmes

Lucy Stensland Laederich

Advocate for Overseas Americans, Free-lance translator,
FAWCO U.S. Liaison and past President
Paris, France

LUCY STENSLAND LAEDERICH, lover of cats and high school Valedictorian, has followed a varied and unusual path as an expat. The daughter of a Swedish father and an American mother lived in Sardinia for a time and attended boarding school in Switzerland for two years, lived in Canada for six years and received her Bachelor's degree from the University of Saskatchewan, but did not become a true "overseas American", as she puts it, until she went to France on a Fulbright grant in 1970, after receiving an ABD (All But Dissertation) doctorate in the History of French Theater from the University of Washington in Seattle. While in Paris, she met and married a French architect, had two children, and created a new life.

Lucy's first job in Paris was teaching English to and coaching high-powered French executives. Then, in 1989, with her children in their teens, she moved into full-time, free-lance translation.

Of her children, she says they are "complex and unconventional: people I am proud to have had a hand in shaping." Her daughter is a musician; her son writes and makes short films and "feels his role in life is consciousness raising." She is happy that both of them - and her granddaughters - live in Paris.

When Lucy became intimately involved with a number of international organizations for which she served in a variety of capacities, including as Vice-Chair of the World Federation of Americans Abroad and President of FAWCO (Federation of American Women's Clubs Overseas), she also became an activist. It was her connection with FAWCO, in fact, that got her active in working on election reform legislation and in the movement to have Americans abroad counted in the U.S. Census, until 2004 when she realized it might well not happen in her lifetime. Regular trips to Washington and an active role in annual "Overseas Americans Weeks" led to her latest endeavor, which has been crowned with some success: the founding of the bi-partisan Americans Abroad Caucus in the House of Representatives, in February of 2007. Membership grew in six months from two to sixteen and the drive continues: the over-arching goal is to advocate for expatriate Americans' voting rights, citizenship rights for spouses and children, fair taxation of overseas Americans and effective, if not Constitutional, representation in Congress of Americans abroad.

Lucy is a force to be reckoned with. She is driven by her desire to "make things better". She is also brilliant, full of energy, and never satisfied with the status quo. Lucy is an example of an expat who successfully adapted to life in her new country but nevertheless works tirelessly as an advocate for her compatriots abroad.

Where there is life there is hope.
Where there is hope there is a will.
And when there is a will there is a way.

All you get is what you give,

                                        so why not give it all.

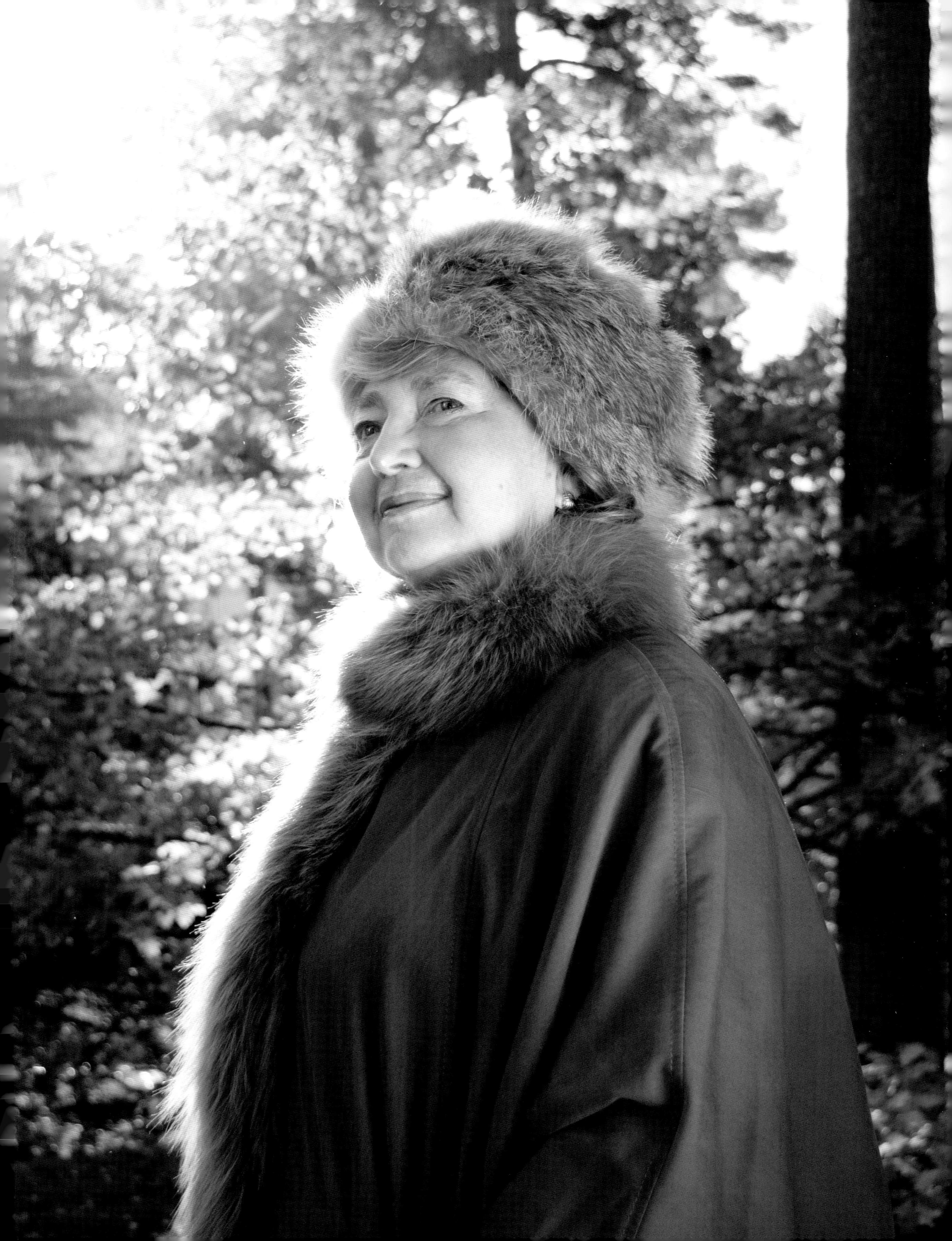

Pearl Lonnfors

University Educator of English for Professional Purposes,
Teacher, Trainer, Translator, Editor,
Helsinki, Finland

PEARL LONNFORS was a young bride when she first arrived in Finland in 1962, and all she remembers of that summer are "three sunny days and a Helsinki populated by people dressed in gray, black, or navy raincoats." Still, she found it all new and exciting. She had met her Finnish husband two years earlier on a blind date, when he was studying journalism at Syracuse University. He later became a diplomat, and they lived in Stockholm for three years and in Washington, DC for three years. Two of their three children were born in Finland, one in the U.S. They now live only minutes away, with their families, often coming home for Sunday brunch, carrying on an American tradition. This is what makes Pearl happiest, having her family around her. Her own childhood was somewhat complicated: Pearl's Polish-Jewish mother died when she was only ten months old, her step-mother was a Chilean Catholic with strict religious convictions, her father was Greek Orthodox from Cyprus, and the family environment was working class, politically aware, left of center. Her first exposure to another culture was from her step-mother, who taught her a new language, a new culture, new dances, new music, new food. "Both Cypriot and Chilean backgrounds define me. My father's influence for my interest in politics and my leftist views, my mother's for my fluency in Spanish and my interest in Latin American music and dance." Married to a well known Finnish news media executive, who is also the author of books and plays, Pearl was an educator and an administrator for the English Section of the University of Helsinki Language Center. In fact, she considers her most significant accomplishment to have worked with an enthusiastic team of colleagues to set up the English program from the start. When, the University Language Center was established in 1977, she was honored to be invited to join the team to develop materials for courses and programs in different fields (Law, Medicine, Journalism, for example), to enable students to function as professionals in English. Within five years, all the University departments had such courses. Pearl herself taught law, journalism, education, and social science students, and eventually went on to train teachers. Her administrative tasks included coordinating the English-speaking staff of 25. Although she retired at 63, she continued to do translations and to edit doctoral theses and books. She has also been active in research projects involving new exchange programs for students and teachers of the EEU. So an American of mixed cultural parentage and upbringing became the "mother hen" of a Finnish family, contributing as well to the educational system of her adopted country, and, in addition, to the educational system of the new Europe.

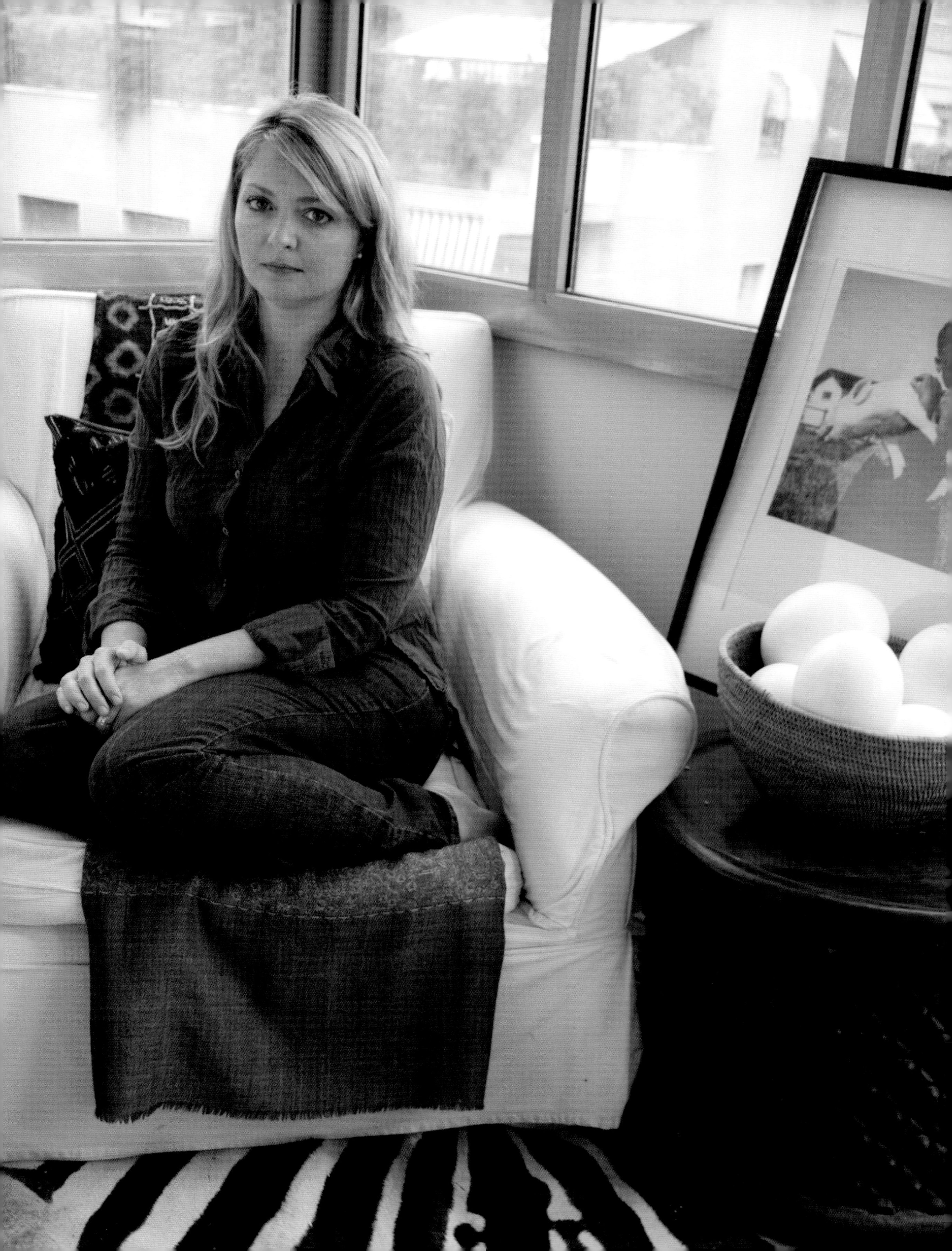

be aware
stay balanced
let go
let be

GILLIAN MCGUIRE is the youngest, but hardly the least accomplished, of the examples chosen for this book. She went to Africa on her own, only weeks after graduation, because she had had an interest in that continent since childhood. In fact, her husband claims that he married her because he was impressed with her bookshelf, filled with books about Africa. She went first to the southern highlands of Tanzania with Operation Crossroads, to spend the summer working on a volunteer community development project. After returning to Washington, her zeal for Africa more than a little inflamed, she worked there for Africare, an American NGO. Two and a half years later, having spent too much time out of the continent that continued to intrigue her, she moved to Niger (West Africa) on the edge of the Sahara Desert, as the deputy there. And that's where she met her American husband, who was working on a U.S. Government project. They were married in a romantic beach ceremony in Benin, a fitting storybook wedding for a woman entranced with a continent from youth. She continued to live in Niger for four more years and to work as the American Ambassador's Self-Help Project Coordinator, then for Lutheran world Relief, primarily with nomadic groups from the far north of Niger. Later, the couple moved to Zimbabwe, with their young son Noah. Living in a dutch gabled house under the shade of thorn acacia trees, she worked to improve the lives of African women. And so she began to help them market the crafts that they were known for, first in Zimbabwe and then abroad. After 15 years in Africa, the McGuires now live in Rome, but their hearts are still in Africa. Gillian misses it (she says she lives with a "yearning for Africa in her soul") and she continues to work on the marketing of the Zimbabwean women's crafts all over the world. This is a woman whose life was changed by her experience abroad and who in turn changed the lives of the people she lived amongst.

Gillian McGuire

Development aid worker, Africa enthusiast
Rome, Italy

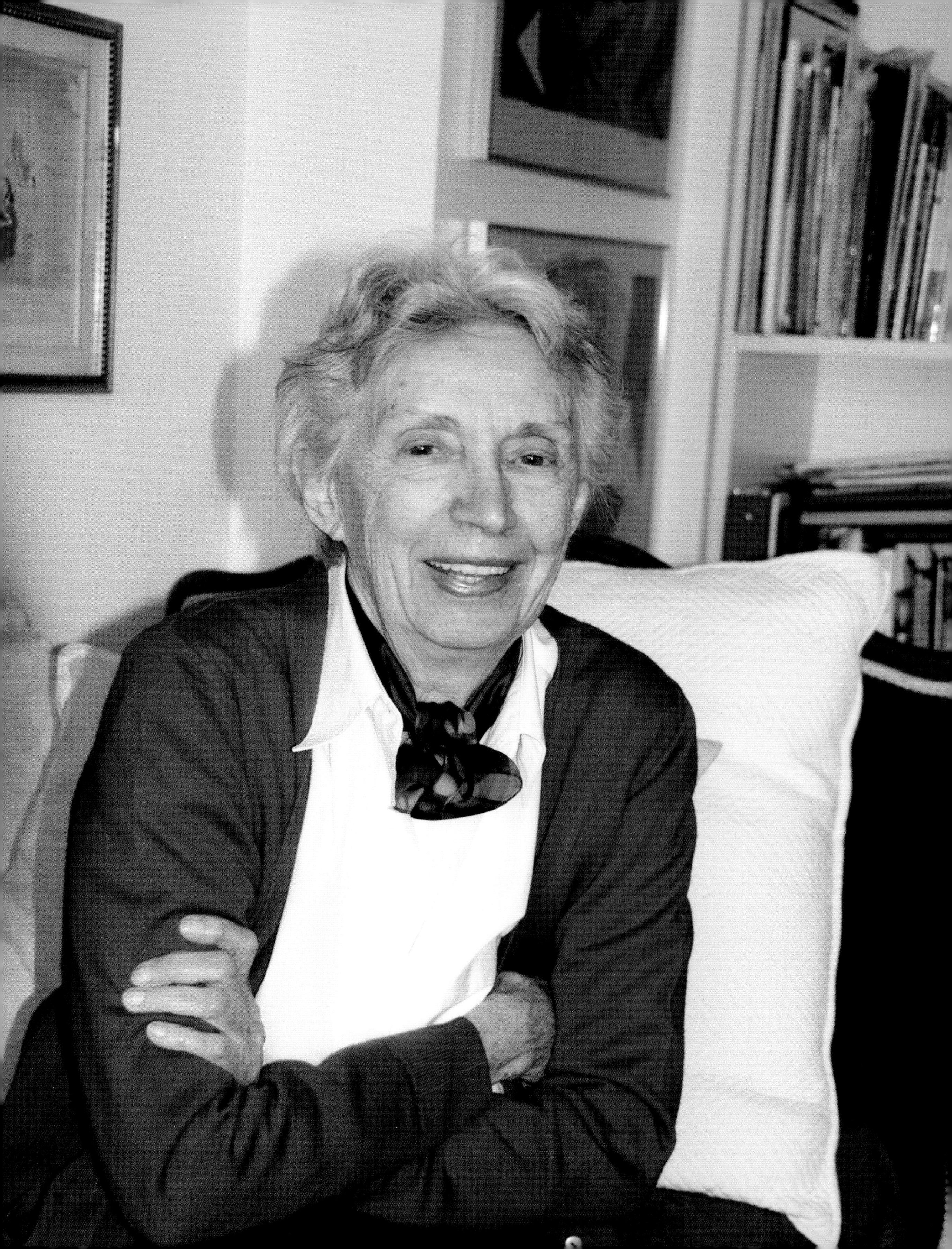

Keep moving

Phyllis Michaux

Author, Advocate for Overseas Americans
Paris, France

PHYLLIS MICHAUX is an expat who has worked on behalf of her fellow Americans even as she leads the life of a French wife and mother. Although petite, she has the strength of her convictions, that the rights of American citizens should be maintained during their period of residence overseas. These include American citizenship for children of American parentage born abroad, equitable tax treatment, certain social benefits including Medicare, and the continued improvement of regulations with regard to absentee voting. She believes that when the image of the expat citizen has changed for the better, laws and regulations will do the same.

It's all there in her book, "The Unknown Ambassadors" (1996) that describes the seven million Americans who reside overseas, and who in their daily lives act as unofficial representatives of the United States . Along the way Phyllis was an early member of the Association of American Wives of Europeans as well as the Association of American Residents Overseas.

Now 85, she is retired, but is still busy at her computer everyday, still passionate about U.S. citizenship issues. Phyllis is a warm and caring person who must be smiling wide inside for all she has accomplished.

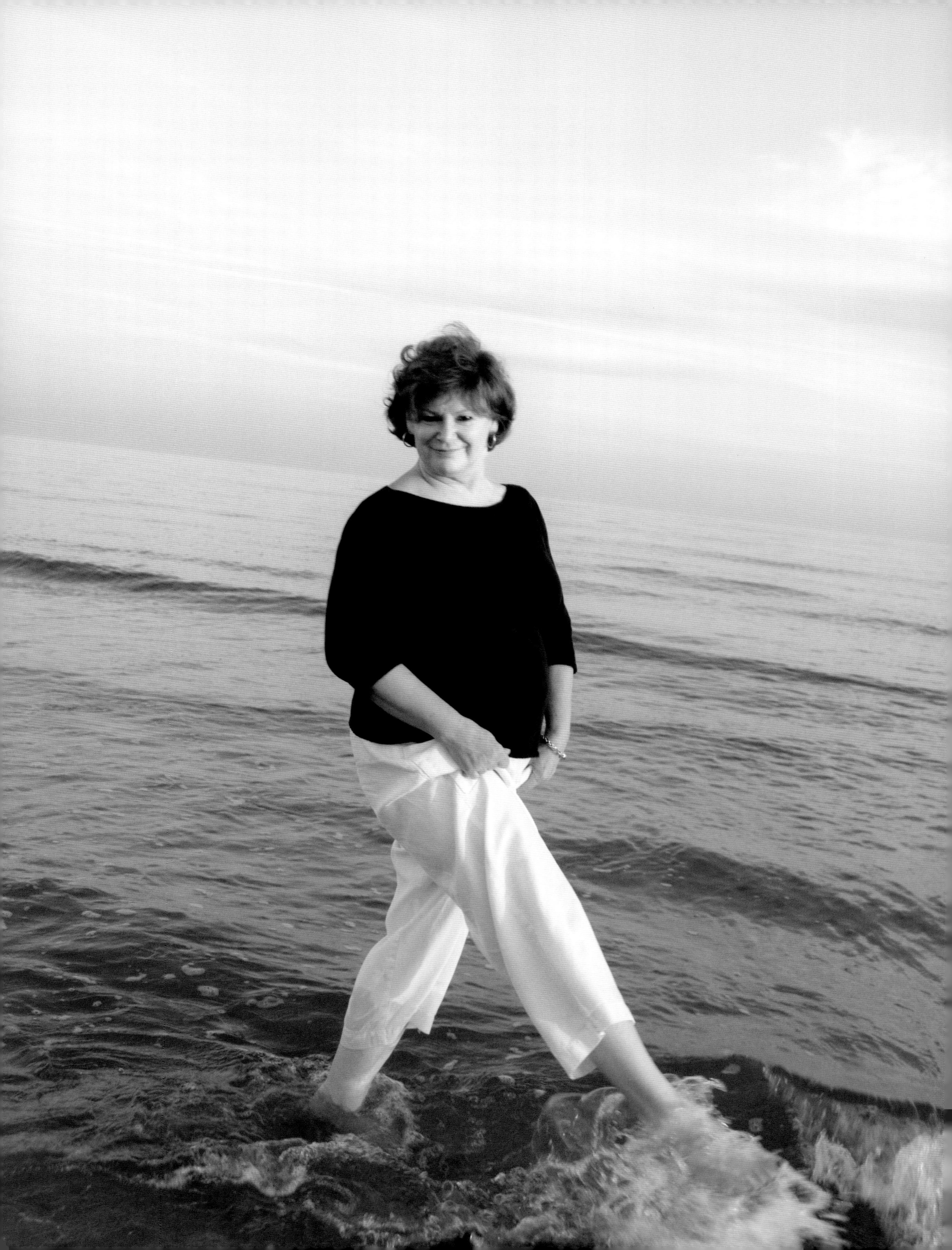

To exist is a fact, to live is an art.

CAROL MIMRAN, using her American ingenuity, her innate smarts, and her strength of character, was able to reinvent herself according to what life threw at her. After graduating from high school, she went with her parents to live in Singapore and in Malaysia for two years where she found work at the American Embassies. She then came back to the U.S. to live and work in Washington as an assistant to a lobbyist. Before the stint in Washington she spent 9 months in Boston where she went often to hear the Boston Symphony. While standing in line for rush tickets she met her future French husband, with whom she moved to France at the age of 23. She has lived there for almost 35 years, by her own admission, doing nothing but being a wife and mother. She chose to remain in her adopted country even after divorcing her husband eight years ago. That's when she emerged and went looking for something meaningful to apply her energies to, to do something for someone else. She found it in teaching adult Arab women in France how to read and write French and in working with ENVIE, an organization helping victims of AIDs live better lives. Carol's jobs with ENVIE are many, but the most important is assisting one of the psychologists to support and animate the Women's Group. This entails monthly meetings and/or workshops, sharing outings to the theater, museum, cinema or any other activity that stirs the interest of the group, and two weekend retreats each year. The group has become "family" to the women in it and has motivated them to make goals for the future and provides strength through the intimate sharing of their particular situation, all of which gives Carol a great deal of satisfaction. Of both of these groups of people she is helping, she says, "They are people I would never have had the good fortune to meet under normal circumstances. For most of them, life's cards were stacked against them. They make me realize that no matter how different another person may be, it's worth the effort to scratch the surface and uncover the soul beneath." She has dedicated herself to these volunteer jobs with gusto and love, and, like the motto of the first FAWCO conference she attended, "bloom where you are planted," she bloomed. Carol enjoys having friends with varied interests (literacy, culture, sports, cooking) and from varied backgrounds, and is happiest when her dining table is surrounded by good friends. She is proud of her children, "her finest accomplishments," she calls them, because they have grown into young adults who care about their fellow man. She is proud of having given some Arab women a bit of dignity through the simple act of learning how to read and write. She is proud of being able to sink herself into a foreign environment and create a full life for herself. Carol is a prime example of an expat woman who learned how to reinvent herself and in so doing made a huge difference to others less fortunate.

Carol Mimran

Advocate for Literacy and ENVIE volunteer,
Languedoc-Rouissillon, France

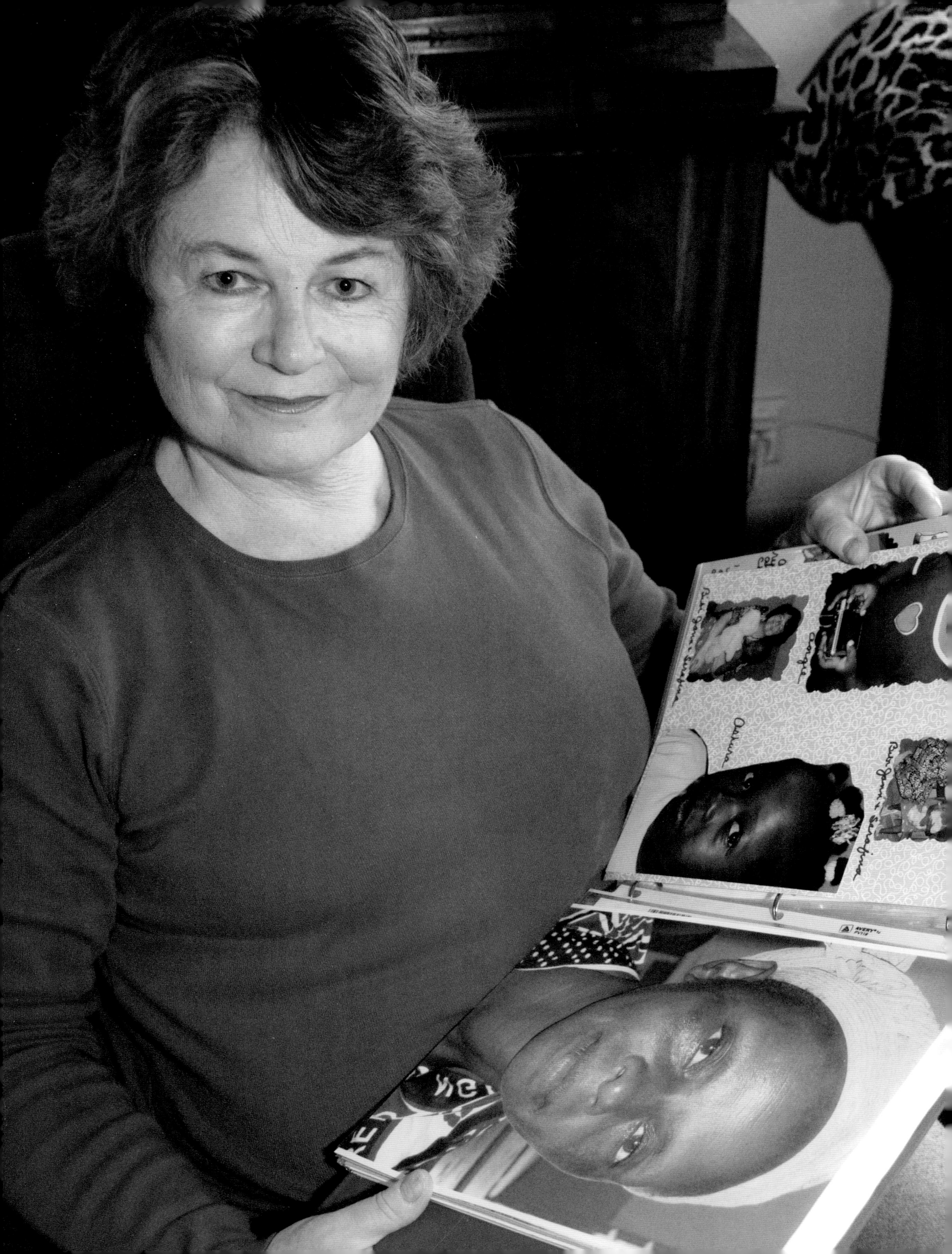

Life is short, but wide – live it!

wide

Jann Mitchell-Sandström

Founder of Bibi Jann Children's™ Care Trust, Author
Stockholm, Sweden

"Life is short - but wide," says JANN MITCHELL-SANDSTRÖM, founder of the Bibi Jann Children's Care Trust in Tanzania, East Africa. Her life and expat love story testitify to that. The Oregon journalist first met Eric, a Swedish physician, in 1978. They lost track of one another for 20 years, but re-located each other over the Internet in 1999. "We were both available and looking for the other," she says. At 55, she took early retirement, moved to Stockholm and married.

With monetary donations from weddings in the U.S. and in Sweden, she built a school for AIDS orphans and poor children near Dar es Salaam, Tanzania, where Eric had worked for years with HIV/AIDS. As a child, Jann had dreamed "day and night" of seeing the world, and now she was able to continue her world travels with Eric. Devastated by the plight of Tanzanian women who had lost their husbands and adult children to AIDS and were forced to rear their orphaned grandchildren on less than $1 per day, Jann expanded the trust beyond the school and small orphanage to include GRANDMA-2-GRANDMA. She finds sponsors world-wide to help the bibi-headed families (bibi is Swahili for grandmother) and aids them in creating crafts to sell.

Now Jann spends most of her time raising money for the project - including creating and selling African wall hangings - and overseeing the trust's website. She's also a feature writer and columnist for a Swedish quarterly and a contributor to a monthly guide in Tanzania. The author of four books (another childhood dream had been to write one book), she also contributes to popular anthologies such as the Chicken Soup for the Soul series.

She boasts of having 208 grandchildren: 8 American, 2 Swedish, and 200 Tanzanian. And she savors the miracle of re-discovering Eric and being - on her third try - "deliciously married."

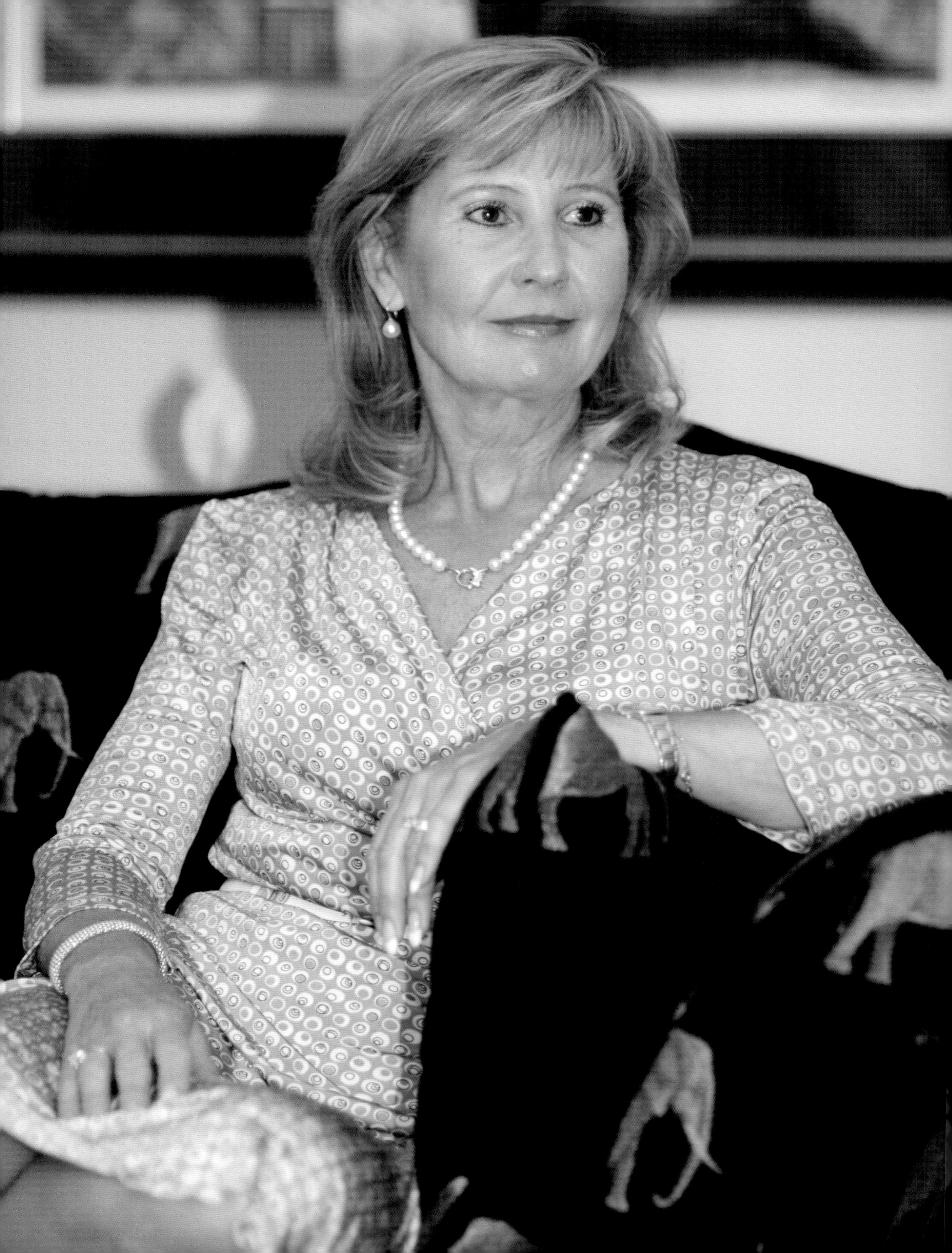

*Any person can have a vision:
it takes an entire group
   to make the vision a reality.*

PAMELA MUSSELMAN, a registered nurse by profession, with a specialty in Emergency Medicine, sold the business she had founded, a nurses' registry to provide temporary staff to emergency departments in Bay Area hospitals, packed up her children, and moved to Budapest to join her husband in 1992. A typical "trailing spouse," she learned early into "this adventure" that international women's volunteer organizations are an important way to understand and appreciate a country.

Pamela chose not to pursue her nursing career overseas, because of language barriers, and instead volunteered for projects connected to the countries where she lived. A self-confident woman with strong leadership skills and a passion for helping people, she has served on the boards of the International Women's Club Foundation of Budapest, the American Women's Association of Vienna, and the American Women's Club of The Hague, where she now lives. After her youngest child was born in Budapest, Pamela gave up the life of a trailing spouse and became an active volunteer in philanthropic fundraising, continuing this endeavor in moves to Brazil and Austria, and now in the Netherlands.

After serving as a member of the planning committee of the Pink Gala, an annual event to raise funds for breast cancer research, education, and advocacy, Pamela volunteered to be co-chair of the event, and it is through her hard work, creativity, and vision that the venue became more impressive, the number of participants grew larger, and Dutch corporate sponsorship expanded.

As President of the American Women's Club of The Hague, she continues her interest in the fight against breast cancer in the Netherlands, and the AWC of The Hague became the driving force behind the launch of the breast cancer awareness campaign in Holland. In fact, since the inception of the AWC fundraising campaign in the spring of 2002, the AWC has donated over 800,000 euros to breast cancer organizations in Holland, and the Pink Gala has become embedded into The Hague's cultural calendar, all as the result of the dedicated efforts of an expat committed to making a difference.

Pamela Musselman

International Fundraiser
The Hague, The Netherlands

Happiness is the ray of sunlight that comes through the cloud.

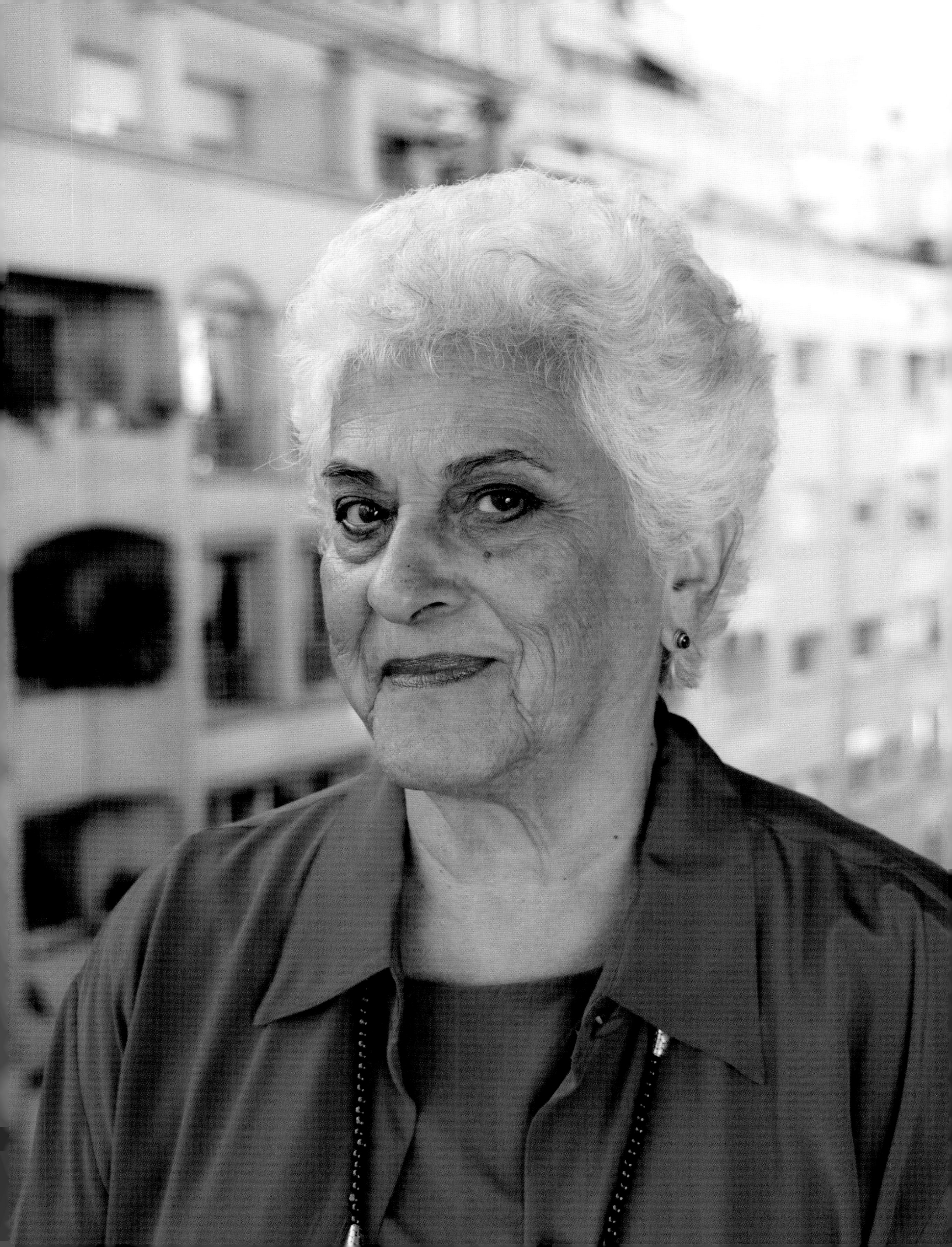

Stella Politis Fizazi

Humanitarian Educator
Casablanca, Morrocco

Although born in the USA, STELLA POLITIS-FIZAZI's Greek ancestry has always played a defining role in her life. Brought up by her mother to understand the importance of her Greek heritage and language, she remembers also what her father found when he first came to the U.S. – signs that said "No dogs or Greeks allowed." Nevertheless, he fought in the American Army in World War I, and Stella believes herself truly American, but, like so many others, an American with foreign roots. Perhaps that's why she found it relatively easy to marry a Moroccan exchange student and go to live with him in his country. There she adapted to still another culture and learned to be so comfortable in it that she was able to accomplish so much there. In 1960s America, both she and her husband were avid "marchers" for many causes; he still calls her "a bleeding heart." She went to Brazil on a scholarship for two years, where she spent her time playing the guitar and dancing, and she still loves to play her beloved 30-year-old guitar. Then, she and her husband moved to Casablanca 44 years ago. Stella started teaching English at the American Language Center, but, natural leader that she has always been, she soon became so involved with the importance of the Center that she had to do more than teach. In fact, she was instrumental in leading it to grow from three to seven centers all over the country, and from 300 to 4,000 students by the time she retired. And then, this American/-Greek/Moroccan became the first American president of the very British Churchill Club in Casablanca. Following in their parents' liberal footsteps, her daughter is now at work in a non-profit NGO in Washington and her son is a human rights lawyer in New York City. Although the successful growth of the American Language Center is her proudest achievement, Stella feels that the role of family, learned from her mother, is the most important aspect of her life, and she is happy that her father was able to spend the last days of his life with her in Casablanca.

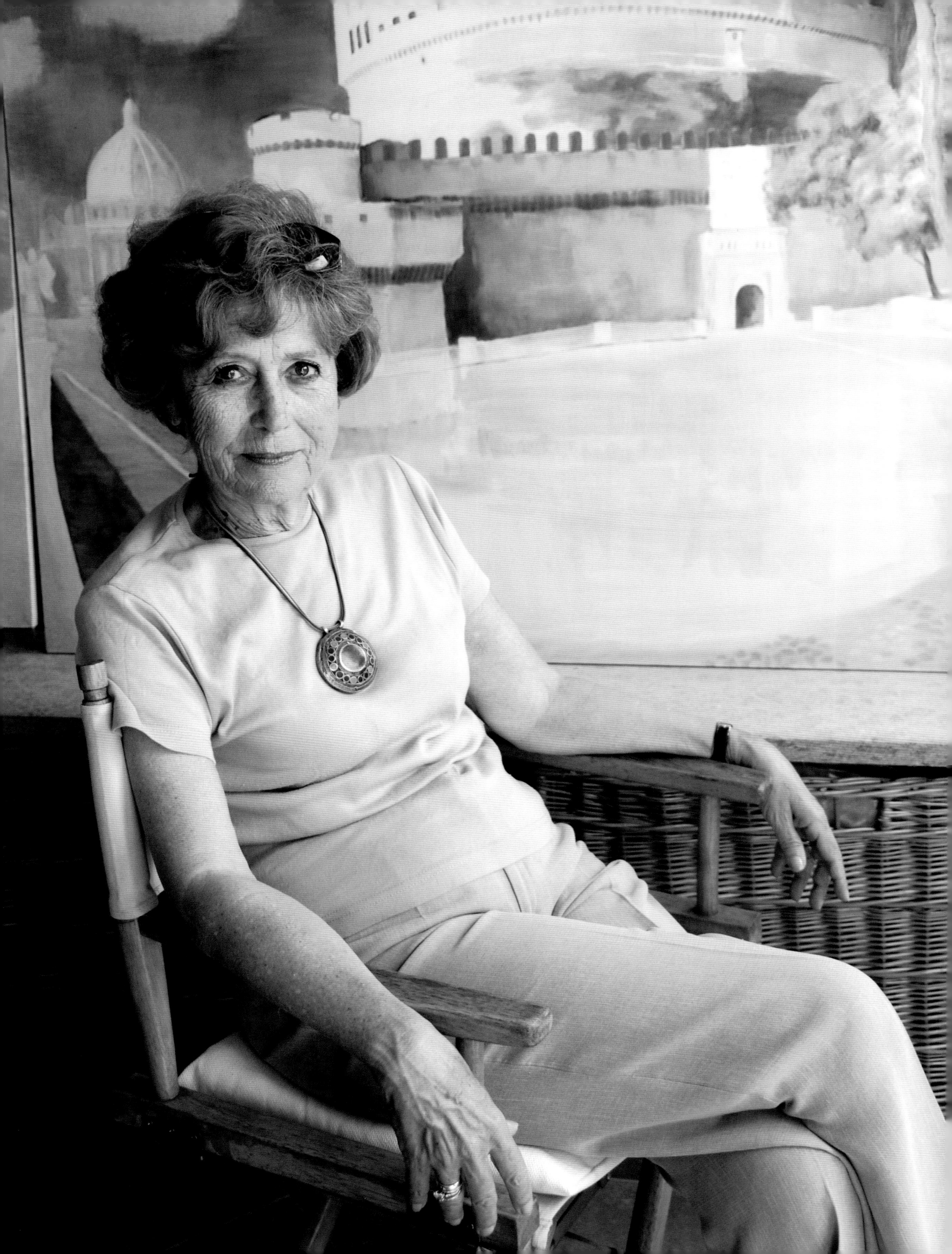

Living is giving. Give your best, live your best.

A successful working artist, with paintings in private collections, ANNE PONTI-RIGGINS is also known for her groundbreaking work in the care of Alzheimer's patients in Italy, where she has lived for 50 years, since marrying her Italian politician husband. She says, "I came to Rome to study at the Academy of Fine Arts for a year and stayed for a lifetime." Her art career has seen many phases, from printmaking and graphics, to etchings and aquatints, to large canvases in oil, which is her current specialty. In addition to producing works of art, Anne began volunteer work while her three sons were growing up in Rome and attending traditional Italian schools. Working with other parents, she organized programs at the schools to coach soccer teams and to provide field trips, until, finally, one evening in her dining room, a "constitution" for an Italian PTA was signed by a headmaster, a faculty representative, and herself an AMERICAN mother. Anne continued to nourish the fledgling organization until it grew to become a national institution.

When her sons finished school, Anne turned her volunteer efforts to health-related fields, advocating for a variety of causes until she stumbled upon Alzheimer disease and realized that in Italy there was nothing to help people cope with this "plague." An ironic footnote to the latter is that it was only two years later that her own husband was diagnosed with Alzheimer. During this difficult time, with the aid of generous, faithful friends, and with help from their three sons, she managed to struggle through the next few years. Anne had to find gainful employment, even while she spent "the 36-hour day" caring for her increasingly debilitated husband. After his death, she continued her fight to have Alzheimer officially recognized as a disease and thereby incorporated into Italy's National Health Service. But still there was no support, no daycare centers, no assistance for families at all. Anne persevered; she helped a voluntary organization plan the first Alzheimer conference in Italy, and from there, painfully slowly, progress began.

With Anne's help, support groups for families were organized, as well as psychological and legal counseling for them, support for research programs, geriatric and neurological assistance for patients, occupational therapies were begun to help patients reinforce their residual capacities thus improving their quality of life. Anne herself translated the American written material to inform and train families, volunteers, care-givers, health professionals, and social workers. These efforts eventually turned into a network throughout Italy of 50 daycare centers where Alzheimer patients can find comfort and courage and care through physical and creative activities, mental exercises, medical supervision, art and music therapies prolonging and fulfilling their "good" years. And now, thanks to the hard work and commitment of an American volunteer residing in Rome, Italy is exporting its training programs to other countries. This volunteer, Anne Ponti-Riggins, has single-handedly made a difference not only to Italy, but to Alzheimer sufferers throughout the world.

Anne Ponti-Riggins

Artist, Founder of PTA Italy
Founding member Alzheimer Association Italy,
Rome, Italy

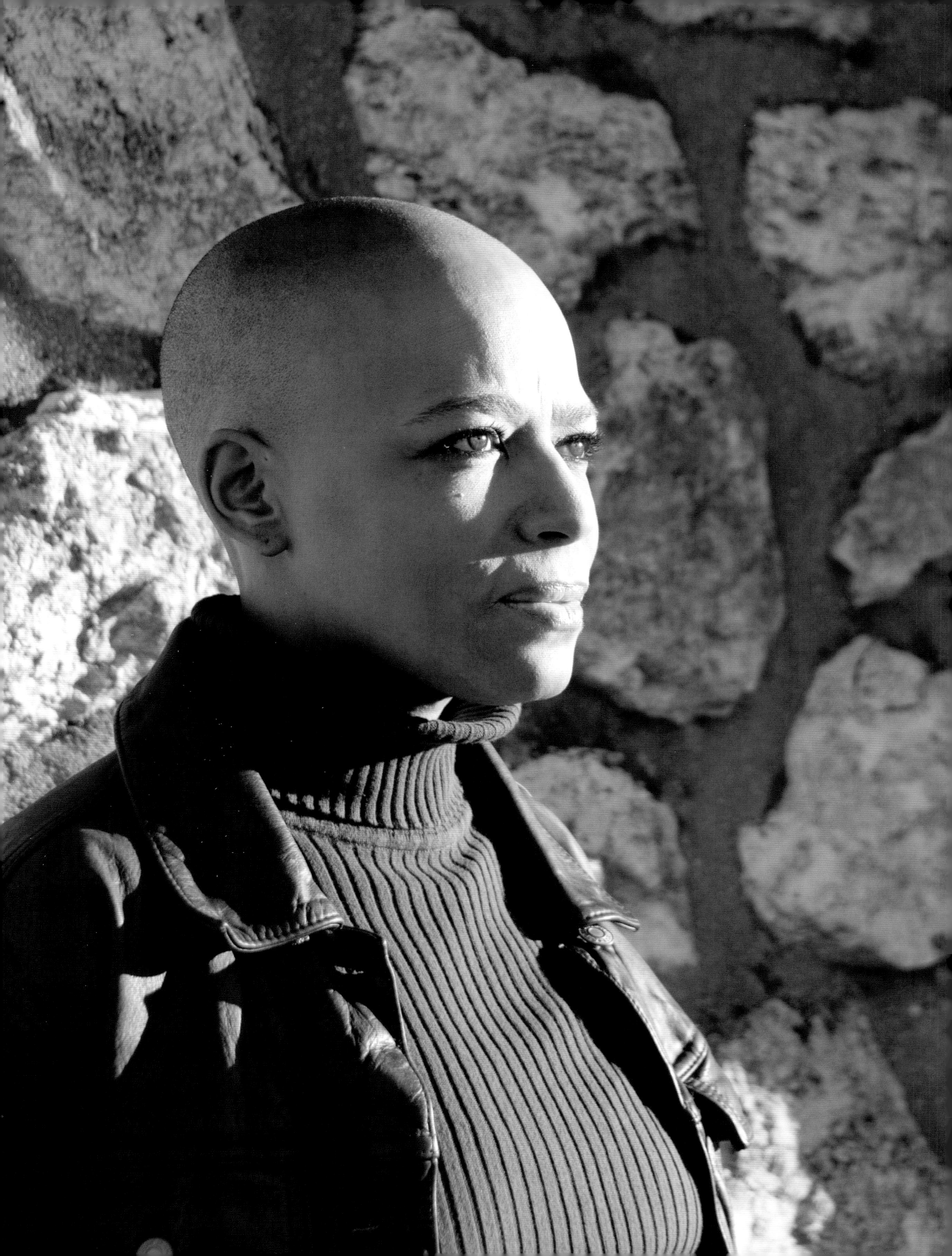

Find your joy.

Kim Powell

Photographer, Community Leader
Paris, France

KIM POWELL's life is and always has been a life of giving, a life of volunteering, and she has done much more than one ordinary person's share of caring and giving. But who said Kim is ordinary? She is a super-active volunteer with myriad responsibilities in many different kinds of organizations. She is a true community leader. And let's not forget that Kim has accomplished all this in a foreign country.

She is a third-term President of the Association of American Wives of Europeans, an organization with 600 members. She is past president of both USA Girl Scouts Overseas and the Sisters Association. Her involvement in these groups was a result of her living in Paris and looking for ways to do volunteer work. She is also a Board member of many other organizations.

She has so many activities and is so busy that she sometimes stops and asks herself „Why?"The answer she comes up with is that she learned the importance of giving back to the community at a very early age as hers was a family of ministers whose commitment to helping those around them has stayed with her through adulthood. She hopes that she can carry on that legacy.

Whatever the underlying reason, people speak of her as „natural leader" and look to her for advice and mentoring. As if that is not enough, she is also a professional photographer, whose art photography has been exhibited many times in France. You would expect someone with this much vitality to be an extrovert, but Kim is reserved and quiet and thoughtful. She is the epitome of the firm hand in the velvet glove. But she is happiest, she says, when someone she has helped reaches their goals.

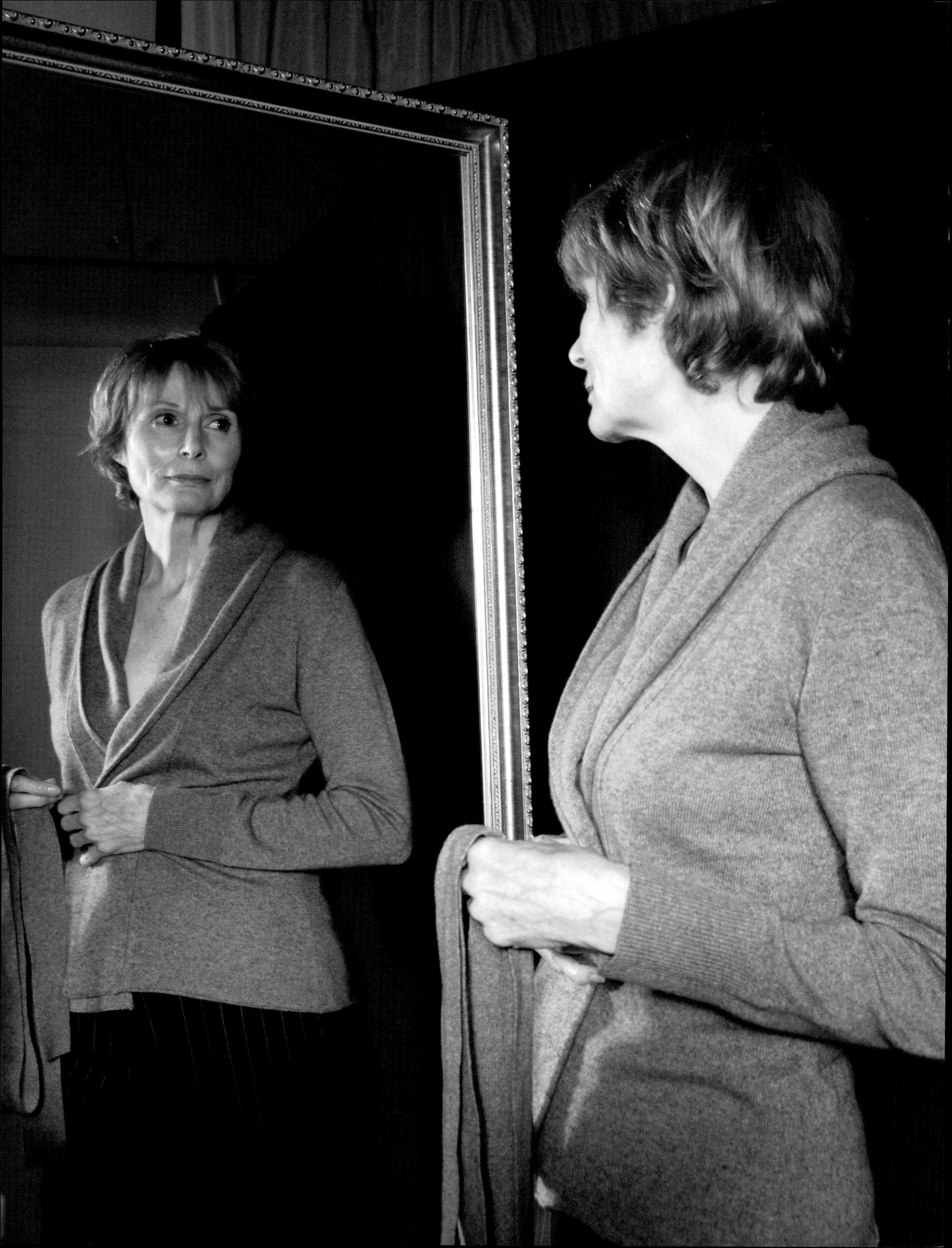

Be grateful for every person in your life and never have regrets!

ADELE RIEPE's story is one of constant adaptation to change. Having lived in Germany (Munich, Wiesbaden, Bonn, and Hamburg) and New York on and off since 1961, her life has changed many times with the years and the cities; some things happened to her, some things she made happen, and always she survived in a new way. Adele has always been astute enough to know how to reinvent herself with the circumstances she finds herself in.

After two husbands, both German, she now lives alone in a small but beautifully decorated apartment in Hamburg. She describes herself as self-critical and terrible with money, but loving and passionate. She is also warm, smart, funny, intelligent, articulate, and has lots of energy. Adele started out as a model moving to Munich in 1961 and working throughout Europe for three years. Realizing that modelling (not so lucrative in those days) was hardly a career, she moved back to New York, becoming Director of Public Relations for Glamour Magazine, and enjoying the "great New York life". There she met her first husband, a well known German television personality. They had a lot in common and were well suited and Adele moved with him to Wiesbaden. She still mourns this first marriage of only five years and she remained good friends with her ex-husband until his death. After her divorce in 1970, she married another German and moved with him to Bonn where she became Bureau Manager of the New York Times, a job she loved. The marriage lasted for 23 years and produced a daughter.

In 1995 Adele moved back to New York ("for good" she thought) where she continued working for the Times. And then her daughter, who had been diagnosed with Multiple Sclerosis at 25, married a German from Hamburg and gave birth to a daughter in 2001. Adele decided she would be needed in Germany.

Now this attractive former model, who used to hobnob with celebrities in her previous incarnations, lives a quiet life as a teacher of English for adults, a career she began at 69. At 70, Adele is still slim and beautiful. She writes film reviews for english publications, teaches, goes to Film festivals and helps her daughter with six-year-old Finya. She is proud of the fact that she has never hesitated to take on any obstacle and invent her life anew so many times.

Adele Riepe

Model, Journalist, Editor, Teacher, Film Critic,
Hamburg, Germany

*When you're open and generous,
you can connect with any human being
beyond anything you might think
would separate you from him or her.*

*You can be active, effectively,
leave an impact wherever you are
if your heart is in it and you embrace
your surroundings.*

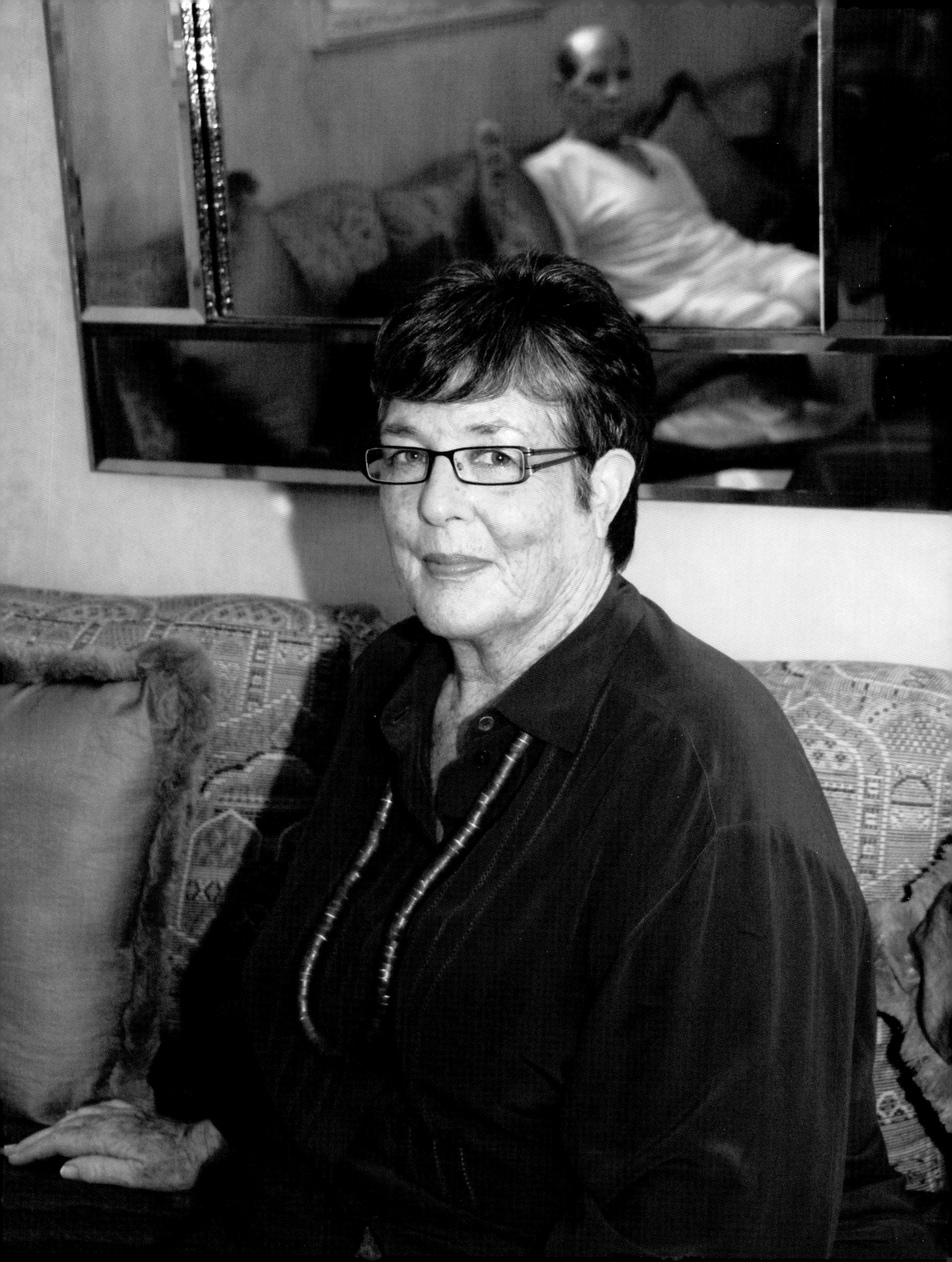

Donna Sebti

Humanitarian
Casablanca, Morrocco

DONNA SEBTI is a 70-year-old humanitarian with a strong personality. That's how her children describe her. An adventurous young Californian, Donna first came to Europe in 1957, on a student tour, liked what she saw and stayed on. After a few months in France, she moved to Spain where she studied at university in Madrid and taught English in a private school for two years. A summer vacation in Morocco ended in her very happy marriage to a Moroccan nearly 50 years ago. Their four children all studied in American universities and spent various amounts of time in the U.S. but they have all returned to Casablanca, to be close to home and family. They are proud of their American mother's openness to other cultures, of her generosity and total dedication to helping those less fortunate, from the sick and disabled, to orphans, and lepers, especially children. Donna is committed to her own children and 9 grandchildren, encouraging them to travel and discover the world just as her own mother did.

Donna began working in Morocco by organizing English classes in a USIS school, then worked for the Moroccan National Airlines as director of language courses and special training for 33 years. Meanwhile, she kept busy with her humanitarian projects. Donna believes in people, and people believe in her; they seek her out for help and guidance.

One of her most ambitious projects was when one of her former students became paraplegic due to a traffic accident, they set out to found an association for the disabled in Morocco. Later thanks to telethons, other fund raisers and philanthropists, their association went on to build a large rehabilitation center where the poor can obtain free operations and the physical therapy they need as well as training when possible to integrate into the work force.

Donna was on the Executive Committee of Family Planning for many years, worked with craftswomen in a shanty town trying to find markets abroad for their arts and crafts and improve their living conditions. Recently she took her grandchildren to distribute over one hundred school bags to young children living in a shanty town. Their parents are largely unemployed, former farm workers from the rural exodus. When she asked the kids what they wanted to be when they grew up, they answered pilots, doctors, school teachers, a judge. Tears came to her eyes as she realized that they might not have beds but they can have dreams.

It is this and other anecdotes, as well as her daily walk along the beach, that keep Donna inspired to continue her good work, even now as she has had to cut back some of her activities to care for her husband, who is gravely ill. Donna is an American expatriate who has made a tremendous hands-on difference to her Moroccan communities.

"Find your purpose in life and make a difference in the world around you."

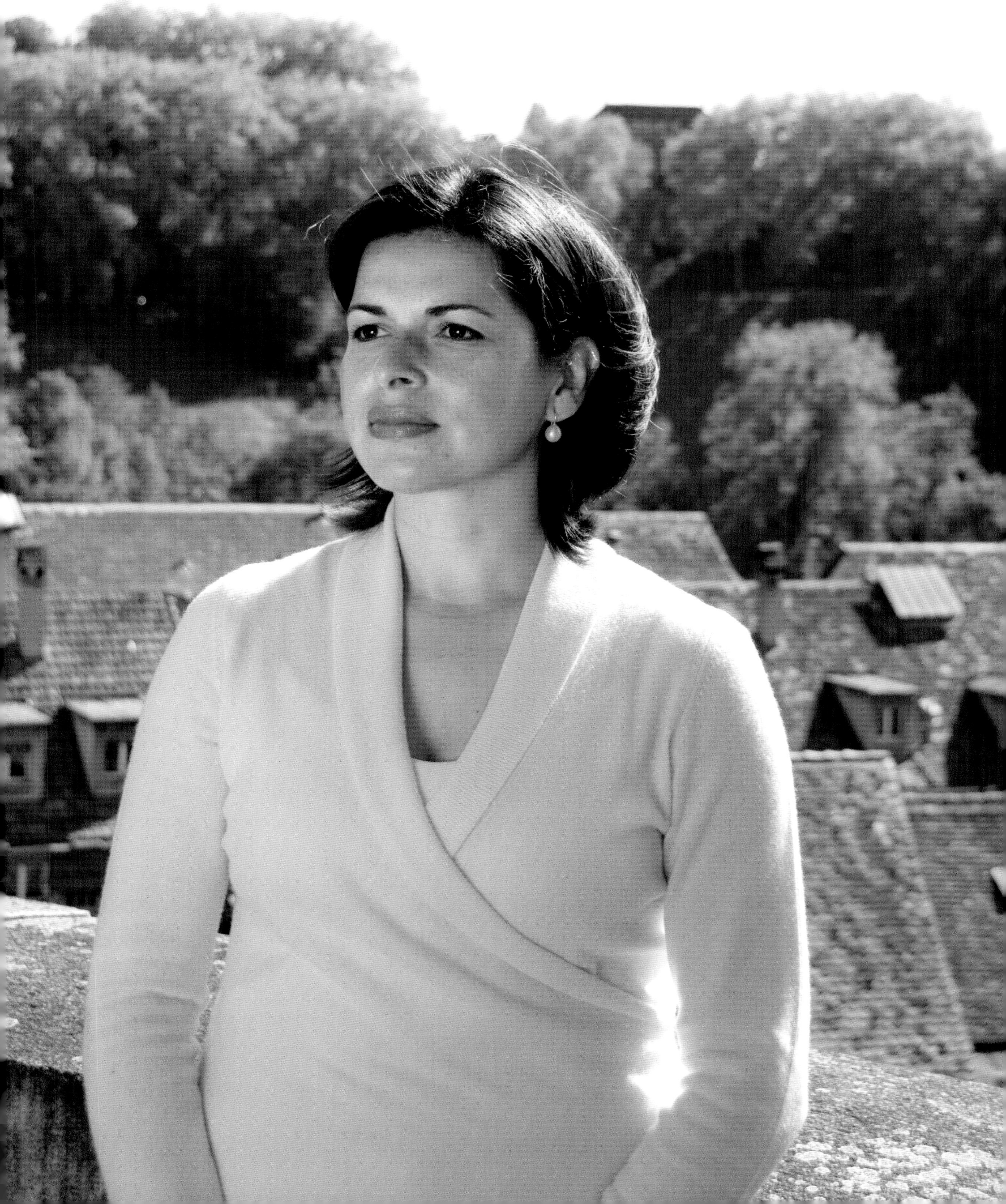

SARA VON MOOS believes that we are all born with a God-given purpose which we are meant to cultivate for our personal fulfillment as well as for the benefit of mankind. "Your purpose in life is what you dream about when you're awake, that which makes you smile and your heart skip a beat whenever you think about it. Simply put, your purpose in life is where your heart is." Sara has found her purpose and happiness in helping those who are less fortunate and is actively engaged in this endeavor at all times.

Sara is Mexican-American, was born in Texas, and grew up in Chicago. She was having a successful career in international sales when she met her Swiss-American husband and moved to Europe. They have since lived in Vienna, Moscow, Oxford, Lubumbashi (Democratic Republic of the Congo) and are now settled in Bern, Switzerland with their two children.

As someone who easily adapts to new cultural environments and quickly becomes active in the local community, Sara tries to make a difference wherever she goes. As she puts it, "I am trying to live a life that matters, trying to make a difference in the world around me." In Congo, for example, she founded an Education Sponsorship Program for the 'Commune de Lubumbashi,' an orphanage which cares for children who have lost their parents due to war, famine or disease. In Bern, Sara works as a full-time volunteer for the Swiss Red Cross, raising funds through the sale of jewelry donations for the 'Old Gold for Eyesight' campaign, which restores eyesight and hope to thousands of poverty strickened blind people in Asia and Africa. Also close to Sara's heart is the 'Villa Maria,' a women's pension and shelter in Bern, where she helps increase awareness about domestic violence and solicits donations.

Friends describe Sara as having a natural beauty that comes from within. She is guided by her faith and convictions and finds inspiration in her family, describing her proudest achievement as "raising two self-confident, life-loving, kind-hearted, socially-responsible children." Also described as being determined and resourceful, Sara explains it: "I firmly believe that the moment you make a decision to do something, the universe conspires to help you."

When asked how long she plans to continue her humanitarian work, Sara responds that she does not see herself stopping anytime soon, as she seems to find opportunities to help her fellow man everywhere she goes.

Sara von Moos

Humanitarian
Bern, Switzerland

Thank You
for your support of Beyond Borders

Friends

Elizabeth Abbot
AARO (Association of Americans Resident Overseas)
American Women's Club of Hamburg
American Women's Club of Taunus
Ron Anderson
Adrienne Bailey
Karen Bakos
Phyllis Barbe
Benvenuto Club of Milan
Kristine Berger
Barbara Bonner
Eleanore Boyse
Leeanne Bray-Klemusch
Leslie Brockett
Marlene Broemer
Mary Brunowsky
Kathleen de Carbuccia
Helen Ward Car
Sallie Chaballier
Irene Checler
Gerald Colonna
Mylinh Corrado
H. Tracy Frank Coutrix
Priscilla Delas
Allison DeLusque
Kathleen Doherty
Lise Ducrey
Norma Fischer
Thelma Freedman
Emanuela Gaertner
Catherine de Gennaro
Michelle Grams
Louise Greeley-Copley
Andrea Hall
Jocelyn Hamada
Linda Harris
Sara Hartmann
Dianne Henning
Karen Hicks
Carol Hoag
Marline Holmes
Nan de Laubadere
Melanie Le
Cynthia Lehmann
MyVan Loehlein
Ann Lepretre
Wendy Leyland
Nathalie Luu
Liz MacNiven
Lan Manson
Melissa Mash
Kathleen McGill
Uta Menges
Michelle Miller
Jann Mitchell-Sandstrom
Miriam Monnin
Madeline Morrow
Mr. & Mrs. Nguyen Ngoc Phuc
Evelyn Nguyen
Michael Nguyen
Minh Nguyen
Mr. Nguyen Ngoc Linh
Phuoc T. Pham
Mrs. Thu Pham Nguyen
Stella Politis Fizazi
Lynn Poole
Anne Ponti-Riggins
Carla Kewley Potok
Georgia Regnault
Marilyn Richard
Christine Rolland
Myra Sastrarahadja-Mevis
Tricia R. Saur
Ann de Simoni
Cynthia Smith-Ayed
Rebecca Tan
Jennifer Taylor
Kathy Tchalaby
The American Women's Club of London
Janet S. Thieme
Y-Lan Tran
Carol Traut-Bender
Anne van Oorschot-Warwick
Kim Vu
Daryl Farrington Walker
Tazmin Walker
Michaela Walsh
Kathleen H. Waugh
Wayne Zetman

Supporters

American Women's Club of Curacao - Curacao, Netherlands Antille
American Women's Club of Dublin - Dublin, Ireland
American Women's Club of Finland - Helsinki, Finland
Association of American Women of Ireland - Dublin, Ireland
Judith Barret - Paris, France
FAWCO Executive Board 2007-2009
Clydette de Groot - The Hague, The Netherlands
Joanna Gallagher - Dublin, Ireland
Marjorie Gunthardt - Zurich, Switzerland
Linda Harris - Palm Harbor, Florida, USA
International Newcomers Club - Madrid, Spain
Shirley Kearney - Basel, Switzerland
Nancy Koster-Tschirhart - Amsterdam, The Netherlands
Lucy Stensland Laederich - Paris, France
Mr & Mrs Nguyen Ngoc Bich - Springfield, Virginia, USA
Mr & Mrs Nguyen Q. Hung - Fresno, California, USA
Mr & Mrs Nguyen Q. Thong - Great Falls, Virginia, USA
Mr. & Mrs. Binh Tran - Springfield, Virginia, USA
Nancy Brown Negley - Houston, Texas, USA
Nancy Newlove - New York, New York, USA
Alan Ong - Los Gatos, California, USA
Tuan Ong - Coppell, Texas, USA
Ashley O'Reilly - Bern, Switzerland
Gwen Perry - Barcelona, Spain
Carlo Ponti - Paris, France
Kim Powell-Jaulin - Paris, France
Kathleen Simon - London, England
The American Women's Club of The Hague - The Hague, The Netherlands
Emily Van Eerten - Coltishall, Norwich, England
Sara von Moos - Bern, Switzerland
Viorell Ziffer-Arendt - Frankfurt, Germany

Sponsors

AAWE (Association of American Wives of Europeans) - Paris, France
Barbara Oetjen Cocchini - Milan, Italy
Cheryl Koenig - Frankfurt, Germany
Laboratorio Fotosintesis - Madrid, Spain
Embassy of the United States of America - Spain
Embassy of the United States of America - Korea